A Re-incarnation Play

Algernon Blackwood

Pharos Books

ISBN: 978-93-59835-67-9
eISBN: 978-93-59832-16-6

©Publisher

Publisher: Pharos Books (P) Ltd.
Plot No.-55, Main Mother Dairy Road
Pandav Nagar, East Delhi-110092
Phone: 011-40395855, +4049916623
WhatsApp: +91 8368220032
E-mail: sales@pharosbooks.in
Website: www.pharosbooks.in
First Edition: 2024

Printed By: Sushma Book Binding House, Okhla
Industrial Area, Phase II, New Delhi-110020

Karma
By Algernon Blackwood

CONTENTS

PROLOGUE

PRESENT DAY

CHARACTERS

PHILLIP LATTIN (45), British Agent in Egypt.

MRS. LATTIN, his wife (40), mentally and physically ill; a woman of strong personality and exacting.

THE DOCTOR, unpretentious, simple in bearing, gentle in manner.

NURSE.

PROLOGUE

SCENE—*Room in Lattin's London house. Mrs. Lattin lies on sofa. A picture of Ancient Egypt, showing the Nile, palms and temples on wall easily visible to her.*

TIME—*Present day, evening.*

Mrs. Lattin

What time is it, nurse—*now?*

Nurse

Close on half-past five.

Mrs. Lattin

(*With irritability of a sick woman.*) Not later? Are you sure? It's so dark.

Nurse

(*Soothingly.*) The dusk is closing in; I'll light your lamp.

Mrs. Lattin

Half-past five, you said? My husband expected to be back before this. Hasn't he come? The appointment was for half-past two.

Nurse

The Foreign Office takes its time. Mr. Lattin will come to you the moment he gets in.

Mrs. Lattin

You're sure? I thought I heard his step.

Nurse

I'll go and see the moment the lamp is lit. But he never forgets. He always comes in here first.

But he's so long to-day, longer than usual. And he looked so grave, nurse, when he left. He looked worried, I thought. You noticed it?

Nurse

He *is* taken up with these politics just now. It's only natural, considering the crisis in Egypt. But he's always so in earnest, isn't he? I noticed nothing unusual. The Government is lucky to have him at such a time. No one could fill *his* place. (*Brings lamp.*) There's the lamp. Is the shading right?

Mrs. Lattin

Fill his place! No, indeed. Phillip understands the natives better than anybody in the world. And the country too (*wistfully*). If only I could bring myself to go back to Egypt with him. (*Irritably.*) The light catches my eye there. To the left a little. Now to the right. Thank you.

Nurse

The doctors all agree it's best not, don't they? The dry climate—

Mrs. Lattin

It's not that, nurse. Dryness is what I *need*—warmth and dryness. It's something else. Egypt frightens me. I can't sleep there. Dreams come to me.

Nurse

The doctors said it was the effect of the climate on the nerves.

Mrs. Lattin

Oh, I know. I'd face it if I could—another winter. It means so much to Mr. Lattin, doesn't it? Nurse! It's curious—it's strange, don't you think—that Mr. Lattin feels nothing of that *I* feel there? I mean—

Nurse

Hark! I think that's Mr. Lattin's step. I'll go and see.

Mrs. Lattin

It can't be the new doctor, can it?

Nurse

Dr. Ogilvie? Not yet. Six o'clock he was to come. He won't be here before his time. These great specialists are busy men.

Mrs. Lattin

(*Wearily.*) I've seen so many doctors. I hardly feel as if I had the strength for a new examination. Dr. Ogilvie will do me no good.

Nurse

Still you will see him. For your husband's sake.

Mrs. Lattin

Ah, yes, for Phillip's sake. I think my husband's coming, nurse.

(*Enter* PHILLIP.)

Nurse

Good-evening, Mr. Lattin. Mrs. Lattin is a trifle better. I'll leave you for a little, but she must not tire herself. We are expecting Dr. Ogilvie at six.

Phillip

I'll be very careful.

[NURSE exit.

(PHILLIP *comes to his wife.*)

Mrs. Lattin

At last, Phillip. I'm so glad you've come, dear. I've been waiting and longing so. They kept you—but you belong to me, don't you? You're tired, poor old thing. Come to me, Phillip—closer. (*Stretches out hand.*)

Phillip

I *am* a bit late. I'm sorry, Little Child. They kept me, yes. But *you*—?

Mrs. Lattin

I'm well enough to listen. You're back; I forgive you. And it's all arranged as you wished—as you hoped?

Phillip

Sir George was kindness itself—

Mrs. Lattin

You saw the Foreign Secretary!

Phillip

You didn't know I was such a big-wig, did you? It is important, you see, dear. The situation out there is complicated. I've left them in the lurch a little, and my advice—er—my knowledge, Sir George was good enough to say—at such a time—

Mrs. Lattin

In the lurch, Phillip! How in the lurch? You're only asking a longer leave than usual.

Phillip

There, there. I don't want you to worry your dear head with politics. The new doctor will be here any minute now. That's far more important.

Mrs. Lattin

I would rather know exactly. It doesn't worry me.

Phillip

It's all been arranged most satisfactorily, dear; and I'm very pleased. So *you're* pleased with me—eh?

Mrs. Lattin

Phillip—what has been arranged?

Phillip

Sir George was most complimentary. The Government would recognise my services—my long services, he called it. He even discussed with me—asked my advice, if you *must* know the full weight of honour placed upon me!—as to my successor—

Mrs. Lattin

Successor!

Phillip

But, darling, *some one* must fill my place. There must be a *locum tenens*, as they say in the church.

Mrs. Lattin

You've—resigned!

Phillip

Dear one, there was no other way. It's a formality, you see. I can always take it up again where I left it off. Our man in Egypt—just now—must be *there*. He must be on the spot, of course—

Mrs. Lattin

But six months' leave! Surely, six months' leave—

Phillip

Means the entire winter. There, there, Little Child, it's nothing. You must not exaggerate like this. What is my work in Egypt compared to being with you. The doctors forbid you to go out. It's quite simple: I prefer to stay with you. *My* world lies in your heart. I—I can always take up the work again when—when you're better.

Mrs. Lattin

Resigned, resigned! You have actually resigned. Your career—I have broken your career—at last—completely. Is it wrong, then, that I need you so?

Phillip

Hush, dearest—

Mrs. Lattin

You have paid this tremendous price—and I have made you pay it.

Phillip

I wish to be always with you. That is my only wish, my only happiness.

Mrs. Lattin

For my sake you have sacrificed—

Phillip

It's I who am selfish to tire you with all this stupid Government business. There, now; you've talked too much and I have done you harm. There's only happiness in my heart. No more nonsense-talk about sacrifice. You must lie quiet and rest again. I can be always with you.

Mrs. Lattin

Yes, to the end—my end and yours. O God! Why did I not understand before?

Phillip

You must not speak like that. Love—our love—knows no end.

Mrs. Lattin

Oh, I am miserable, Phillip, miserable, miserable.

Phillip

Please, do not say such things.

Mrs. Lattin

But I must, I must. My selfishness has brought you to this last renouncement. Egypt has meant so much to you.

Phillip

Too much, Mary, too much. Egypt was coming between us.

Mrs. Lattin

Your work there, the great work I have ruined…! Egypt meant home to you.

Phillip

Home is where you are, dearest, and nowhere else. You have taught me this—in time. (*To himself.*) Egypt! Ah, Egypt!

Mrs. Lattin

I hate it. It terrifies me. There is pain for me in Egypt. An instinctive dread comes over me always—something from very far away. I **have** struggled against it, for your sake, but—oh, it's so, so strong. If only you could forgive me—!

Phillip

Hush, dearest!

Mrs. Lattin

But it *has* come between us. You love it so. And it's my fault that you can't—your career, I mean—

Phillip

Dear one, whatever is, is right. There is nothing to regret. Egypt, indeed, has drawn me strangely. There is some power out there—a spiritual power—that has cast a glamour over me. It has been a passion with me.

Mrs. Lattin

My instinctive terror!

Phillip

And my instinctive love!

[*They glance together in silence at a great picture above the bed—an Egyptian night-scene, with stars and Nile.*

Yes ... yes ... strange indeed! From my earliest days it drew me. Those palms and temples, that majestic desert—!

Mrs. Lattin

Phillip, don't! Those stars, that river bring me sadness—immense regret. I feel them always rising over me. They watch me!

Phillip

Forgive me. It was the marvellous beauty took me. I—

Mrs. Lattin

But it's an unearthly beauty. And something in it—lost. It's lost to you. And I—oh, but I do love you so; for ever and ever you are *mine*—aren't you?

[*He stoops and kisses her. She half rises, whispering:*

Phillip, dearest—something strange comes over me. I see a lifting of this heavy English sky. I have been through this before—I have done this very thing before—long, long ago—injured you somehow! Oh, Phillip, can it be that we have lived before—pre-existence—is it true? (*Sinks back.*) I think … I think I must be near to … death!

Phillip

Hush, hush, my darling. These are sick fancies only. Your brain is tired. We must not talk like this.

Mrs. Lattin

I **am** tired, yes; but it is my soul that aches and not my body. Phillip, I want your forgiveness.

Phillip

There is nothing to forgive. I love you.

Mrs. Lattin

(*Spiritually tortured and perplexed.*) I want your real forgiveness— before I go. I have been suffering deeply, deeply. Curtains have been rising. I almost see. Something seems growing clearer to me. I've done wrong somewhere! Why have I pulled against you all these years— against your work? It cannot be my love that is at fault. You're wholly mine—and yet I want your forgiveness somehow—

Phillip

(*Deep patience.*) All the love and forgiveness in the world I give you, Little Child. But you ask for what was always yours.

Mrs. Lattin

Your broken mission. You alone have the strength and patience Egypt needs. I have ruined all, all, all!

Phillip

There! I forgive you, then. (*Kisses her.*) I forgive you all, all, all. But please calm yourself. This excitement does you harm. You torment yourself for nothing. It is I who have been, and am, the egoist. All men who think their work is a mission are shameless egoists.

Mrs. Lattin

Thank you, Phillip, for this great gift of your forgiveness. But it is not enough. I want to understand—and so forgive *myself*.

Phillip

You must rest now a little. It was criminal of me to let you talk so much. No, not another word. I'll leave you for a bit. You must be calm to see the Doctor. It's nearly six—

Mrs. Lattin

Dr. Ogilvie can't help me.

Phillip

What! The first man of the day! His wonderful cures—

Mrs. Lattin

He cures the body only. *I* need a soul physician. Oh, Phillip, I believe sometimes my yearning **must** bring him to me.

Phillip

My darling, it is your body alone that is ill. Your suffering gives you these strange fancies.

Mrs. Lattin

You love me too well to understand. (**Sighs.**) My illness is not only of the body. Now, leave me, dearest. I wish to see him quite alone.

Phillip

Little Child, you shall. You can dismiss the nurse. (**Glances at clock.**) It is close on six.

Mrs. Lattin

Kiss me. (**He kisses her softly and goes out.**) If only—ah, if only my great yearning....

[*She lies back exhausted. Sighs. Covers her face with her hands. After a moment she uncovers her face and half sits up again. She stares hard at Egyptian picture on the wall.*

The fault lies in my soul, and it comes first from there—from Egypt. The river is rising, rising once again. The stars are rising too.

They watch me, and they wait. They're always watching us. O God! If only some one could make me understand! If some great doctor of the soul…! (**Sinks back. Her eyes close. She lies very still**.)

[*A big clock on the mantelpiece strikes the first three strokes of six o'clock, then stops. The door opens slowly and a man enters quietly. He looks round the room, sees her on the sofa apparently asleep, and stands still, a few feet inside the door. He looks steadily at her a moment, then glances at the picture of Egypt on the wall. He smiles gently. His figure is a little bent, perhaps. He is not a big man with any marked presence. As he smiles, she opens her eyes and sees him. She shows surprise and slight embarrassment. She raises herself on one arm. Her voice is hushed rather when she speaks. He remains near the open door.*

I beg your pardon. Is it—Dr. Ogilvie?

Doctor

I am the Doctor.

Mrs. Lattin

I must apologise. Did no one—?

Doctor

I found my way.

[*Both pause, gazing.*

Mrs. Lattin

(**With relief.**) Ah! Thank you.

[*She makes an unfinished gesture towards a seat. Her eyes remain fixed on his. She smiles faintly.*

Doctor

You called for me. (*He makes one step nearer.*)

Mrs. Lattin

My husband, I believe, did write. We—expected you.

Doctor

I am come.

Mrs. Lattin

It is exceedingly—it is more than kind of you. You are so good. I mean—(**stammers; sinks back upon the cushions, unable to maintain the effort**). I am very ill.

Doctor

I know.

Mrs. Lattin

You know! Ah yes—you know.

Doctor

That is why you called me. That is why I am here now.

Mrs. Lattin

I can tell you very briefly what—

Doctor

It is unnecessary.

Mrs. Lattin

But—

Doctor

I have been watching you.

[*He straightens up a little; a new dignity is in him. She gazes intently. She stretches out a hand, then withdraws it, hesitatingly, again.*

Mrs. Lattin

You mean—?

Doctor

I knew—that you would send for me.

Mrs. Lattin

Ah! The medical journals! My case, of course—its peculiar—er—its hopelessness.

Doctor

There are no hopeless cases. (*He smiles. His voice is very gentle.*)

Mrs. Lattin

(*Bewildered.*) You are very ki—good. I thank you, already.

Doctor

(*Shaking his head quietly.*) And you already—I see—are on the way to your recovery.

Mrs. Lattin

Recovery!

Doctor

Since you realise that you are very ill.

Mrs. Lattin

Oh—in that sense.

Doctor

In every sense.

[*She is more and more aware of something unusual in him. She keeps her gaze steadily on his face. She makes a gesture towards him, then hesitates. She seems on the point of saying more—speaking more freely.*

Mrs. Lattin

I think—there must be a mistake somewhere. I don't quite understand how you—

Doctor

There are no mistakes.

Mrs. Lattin

But you are sure it is *me* you have come to see?

Doctor

It is you.

Mrs. Lattin

Mrs. Lattin?

[*He bows his head.*

In this street and house—13 Bristol Square?

Doctor

This street, this square (*moves nearer and puts his hand upon her head*), this very house you occupy—for the moment.

[*She stares at him. They smile. She is aware of another meaning in his words. A touch of awe shows in her manner.*

Mrs. Lattin

(*Low.*) This—body?

Doctor

Which, for the moment, *you*—are occupying, Little Child.

Mrs. Lattin

(*Awed.*) You know that name! My husband's secret name!

Doctor

It is—*your* name.

[*He moves back a step so that she can see the picture. One hand he stretches towards her as in blessing. Her eyes turn from the Egyptian night-scene to his face again.*

Mrs. Lattin

(*Softly, to herself.*) My little secret love-name. It is too marvellous—this. I am completely at a loss to—(*breaks off, as he looks down and smiles at her*).

Doctor

Love names truly always.

Mrs. Lattin

He … has … always … called me so.

Doctor

He has loved you truly—always.

Mrs. Lattin

(*Sitting up.*) But you know everything in the world! Who are you— really? (*Awe increases in her.*)

Doctor

I am the Doctor.

Mrs. Lattin

Doctor! The greatest calling in world! A doctor's powers—

Doctor

Are, by rights, divine.

Mrs. Lattin

Life or death—

Doctor

Life *and* death.

Mrs. Lattin

(*Hushed.*) But—you are more than doctor; you are also—Priest.

Doctor

I am at your service.

Mrs. Lattin

(*Light breaking on her face. She stretches out a hand to him. He takes it.*) To heal me. I feel great power pouring from you—into me. It is like wind and fire.

Doctor

Life is a wind and fire. It is life you feel. Your claim is great, because of your great wish, your true desire. You deserve. And I have come.

Mrs. Lattin

(*Puzzled.*) Deserve! My great desire! My claim…!

Doctor

Your sickness is not of the heart, but of the soul. Your desire was prayer.

Mrs. Lattin

You have read my heart.

Doctor

Little Child, it is in your eyes.

Mrs. Lattin

And you know my very soul.

Doctor

Little Child, I am come to heal it.

Mrs. Lattin

Recovery! You said recovery. While I lie dying here by inches!

Doctor

You love.

Mrs. Lattin

With all my heart.

Doctor

And—soul?

[*He looks questioningly down at her with great tenderness. Her expression shows the dawn of comprehension.*

Mrs. Lattin

(*Very low.*) I love—wrongly—somewhere. I forgot—my soul. And I have wrecked him, wrecked his life, his work.

Doctor

(*To himself.*) Again.

Mrs. Lattin

(*Not catching his word.*) Is there recovery for *that*? Can you heal that?

Doctor

He does not question your love for him?

Mrs. Lattin

He is too big-hearted. He has sacrificed all for me. It is regret and remorse that kill me now—they bring death more quickly. If only I could understand!

Doctor

You shall.

Mrs. Lattin

(*Bitterly.*) When it is too late. Can you give recovery for that? Can the forgiveness that I crave—his forgiveness—undo what has been? (*Hides her face and sobs.*) I must die without forgiveness.

Doctor

Recovery begins with understanding.

Mrs. Lattin

I want *his* forgiveness.

Doctor

You must—forgive yourself.

Mrs. Lattin

Oh, oh, I do not understand. My remorse goes with me even into the grave.

Doctor

Remorse brings weakness. The forgiveness of another affects that other only.

Mrs. Lattin

(*Looking up.*) Yes?

Doctor

Understand. Then, without regret, go forward. To forgive yourself is—true forgiveness.

Mrs. Lattin

I feel something wonderful in you. Your words bring life again.... I.... There seems something I remember—remember almost—very dim and far away.... (*Her eye falls upon the Egyptian picture. She gazes fascinated at it.*) The stars ... the river ... are rising, surely....

Doctor

You remember—life. And life shall teach you this.

Mrs. Lattin

Life! My life! Oh, what is it rising in me? A curtain lifts. I see ... myself. Ah, now it goes again.... The pain ... the pain is awful! It all has been before somewhere, I know.… Have I done this before, then? If only I could see, I might understand.

Doctor

You shall see. Understanding shall bring recovery.

[*As he speaks he retires slowly backwards towards the open door. Her eyes remain fixed upon the picture.*

Mrs. Lattin

Recovery! I half remember.… I begin to … understand…!

Doctor

The soul reaps ever its own harvest, for the soul is linked to all its past.

Mrs. Lattin

(*Faintly.*) The past! *My* past…! *Our* past together.…

Doctor

Your pain and prayer may lift for once the curtain. Remembering, you shall understand. And, understanding, you shall learn to—forgive yourself.

[*A light falls on his face and figure by the door. Just before he disappears she tears her gaze away from the picture, and turns to him with outstretched hands. He raises his hands as though he were lifting a curtain and holding it up.*

Mrs. Lattin

It lifts, it lifts! I hear wind among the palms, and lapping waters. A voice is whispering … "Little Child" … yet in another tongue.…

[*From beyond the door his last words reach her with a distant, half-chanting sound.*

Doctor

Egypt! Where you began—with him. Your earliest life. Then other lives as well. See—and understand.

[*She sinks back exhausted. Her face is radiant through her tears. She has just strength enough to touch the pneumatic bell beside the bed.*

CURTAIN

ACT I
THEIR FIRST LIFE TOGETHER.
TIME—2000 B.C.
EGYPT

CHARACTERS

MENOPHIS, a young Egyptian, well born, about 30.

NEFERTITI, an Egyptian dancing-girl.

SETHOS, Egyptian youth.

RAMES, High Priest in Temple of Aton.

•••

ACT I

SCENE—*Banks of the Nile. White temple visible in distance. Kephren's Pyramid seen very far away.*

Late evening, sunset.

(NEFERTITI *and* SETHOS *enter and pause.*)

Nefertiti

Now leave me, Sethos. And go swiftly. (*With gesture of pushing him off.*) I must be alone. You follow me as wind follows a bird.

Sethos

Yet never touch you as wind does the bird. And when you dance your feet dance on my heart. No other dancing-girl compares with you.

Nefertiti

Last moon Pharaoh himself told me that. I know it. But now leave me. I am here to worship.

Sethos

(*Supplicating.*) May I not stay a moment—at least, until Menophis—?

Nefertiti

Sethos, you heard me. It is the sacred night. The tear of Isis falls into our River when the dusk has passed to darkness. And I must worship.

Sethos

Menophis comes also with the dusk. You meet here every evening; and when he comes I am forgotten. May I not stay and be remembered—till he comes? (*Implores.*) Your beauty makes me slavish. Out of his plenty he will not miss so little, and I—starve.

Nefertiti

Not now. Sethos, I tell you, go! His coming, as you know, makes the dry desert live for me. I would not have him troubled for so little. He hardly is aware of your existence—as yet. But, should I ever need you—slave—!

Sethos

(*Eagerly.*) As yet! Need me! Oh, Nefertiti, if you could use me I should die of happiness.

Nefertiti

Then prepare to die, for the time *may* come.

Sethos

Oh, may it happen soon!

Nefertiti

(*Teasing.*) The Gods alone know what may happen, and when. You are my slave. Then, vanish!

Sethos

(*Bowing.*) Your slave obeys. (*Rising.*) But your lover will wait among the palm-trees yonder. Menophis may not come. The Gods know what will happen, and it is said the Gods have claimed him for themselves. He is a prize, it seems, that earth and heaven both desire. I have heard rumours. (*Moves off lingeringly.*) If you need escort back to Memphis your lightest call will reach me.

Nefertiti

Go! I shall not need your escort. My happiness and his are in the keeping of the Gods. Leave me to worship.

Sethos

(*With boy's passion.*) Oh, Nefertiti, the wild sweetness of the desert is in your breath! To me you are holy as our sacred River! May the Gods grant you all your heart's desire. Sethos is your slave for ever—even though his heart should break.

[Exit, slowly, looking back.

Nefertiti

(*Smiling to herself.*) A slave is always useful—for slavish purposes. I may put you to the test some day!

[She watches him out of sight behind the palms, then goes to the water's edge and splashes idly with her bare foot several times in succession, accompanying each splash with a remark.

He'll bury himself in the Temple.... He'll bury himself in my arms.... He'll become a monk at Rames' bidding.... He'll become mine. (*Makes biggest splash of all.*) I've got him ... under this very foot! (*Hears his footstep.*)

Menophis

(Entering.) You here! Nefertiti! (*She pretends not to hear. She is worshipping.*) Nefertiti!

Nefertiti

(*Startled.*) Menophis!

Menophis

You worship here at dusk ... beside the Nile!

Nefertiti

I often come at sunset—as you know.

Menophis

I ... had ... forgotten.

Nefertiti

Forgotten! Has some Afreet blinded you? Only last night, too, you passed me by without a glance—on your way to Aton's new Temple.

Menophis

It was moonless and I did not see you. No Afreet power could hide you in the sunshine.

Nefertiti

(*Mocking*.) Oh, thank you, Menophis. I thought your heart was too full perhaps to see me.

Menophis

You have been worshipping alone—and you were lonely. Forgive me, Little Child, I—

Nefertiti

I forgive you, O handsome Menophis. But I was not lonely. Sethos kept me company awhile.

Menophis

Sethos! The Syrian banker's son! You can find pleasure in such company?

Nefertiti

(*Softly*.) You did not come here to talk with me of Sethos. You came, like me, to worship—!

Menophis

He is rich.

Nefertiti

He is forgotten too. When you call me "Little Child" the whole world is forgotten. There is only—You.

Menophis

Little ... Child.

Nefertiti

(*Goes closer*.) Your eyes seem strange to me to-night: they look far away into space. Your voice sounds distant like the desert jackal's cry. (*She puts a hand on his and looks searchingly into his eyes*.) Yet you call me Little Child, as of old, when we met here every evening in the dusk ... to play and talk and dream together ... of the future. Menophis (*taking his other hand and drawing her body closer to him*), will you not tell me—your Little Child—this sacred night when the Tear of Isis bids our river rise—tell me what wonderful new dream has crept into this faithful heart? (*Lowers her head as though to hear its beating.*) I hear another music in your blood. (*Lifts her face to his.*) And it is … beautiful. (*Waits for his reply.*)

Menophis

It is the Sacred Night. That means—Had you forgotten?

Nefertiti

(*Alarmed, but half teasing.*) Oh, you Solemnity! Forgotten what?

Menophis

(*Gravely.*) A choice—a decision—made to-night is made for ever.

Nefertiti

(*Low.*) I know.

Menophis

Little Child, it is for me a crisis, and I must choose between great issues. My life, too, is rising. I must decide in what direction it shall flow.

Nefertiti

You mean … with whom?

Menophis

For whom.

[*He turns his head a moment towards the distant Temple of Aton, just visible still in the last sunset light. Its whiteness gleams. She notices the gesture.*

Nefertiti

How cold it has grown. Menophis.… I feel the desert-wind's fingers at my heart. It is the North wind from the sea. You, too, seem distant suddenly. (*Lowering voice.*) I fear for you. Why is it? I fear something … for myself … as well—

Menophis

There is no fear this sacred night. There is courage only. Life increases everywhere. The river rises. The Tear of Isis falls into the Nile and—

Nefertiti

Hark! (*She listens.*) There are awful things about in Egypt when—

Menophis

She is alive, that's all.

Nefertiti

Listen!

Menophis

It is the lapping waves. It is the wind among the palms.

Nefertiti

(*Whispering.*) The waters! That cold desert wind! It blows between us—between you and me. There is a shadow! (*Shudders closer to him.*) Surely great Kephren bowed this way!

Menophis

The stars shine over us. They cast no shadow. The pyramid stands fast.

Nefertiti

Yet something passed between us, for I felt it. (*Grips him.*) You are all *mine?*

Menophis

(*Holds her close.*) There is no room. A shadow cannot separate us. Anything *real* would bind us closer only.

Nefertiti

Then why are you so solemn, your eyes so far away, your voice so distant? This crisis that you speak of—it could not take you from *me?*

Menophis

Nothing can take you from me, or me from you—for long. The chain of our past and future lives is bound together beyond all breaking.

Nefertiti

What is it, then, that frightens me?

Menophis

(*With grave tenderness.*) Ah, Nefertiti, Little Child, to-night I stand—
we stand together—at the very gates of life. The choice is difficult, for
it involves you too. Since first, three years ago, I saw you flitting, like a
swallow, down the river bank at Memphis—since those enchanted days
I have had no other human love but you—

Nefertiti

(*Startled.*) No other *human* love!

Menophis

(*Slowly.*) There *is* another love, my Nefertiti—a greater; not more
enduring, perhaps, but nobler. For it demands the greater sacrifice.
And, cold though it seem to your warm, passionate heart—*if* it
should call me—

Nefertiti

(*Catching him by the arm.*) Greater! Yet would take you from me! But
you *are* mine!

Menophis

Your beauty troubles me; my blood rebels. I cannot look at you and
hear the call this sacred night may bring me. I must make a still place for
my soul to listen. (*Slowly.*) Oh, Nefertiti, you must leave me—for a little.

Nefertiti

Not knowing what is in your troubled heart! Not hearing from your
own lips if we shall meet again!

Menophis

(*Sees Rames approaching.*) You should know all. If not from my lips,
then from—

Nefertiti

(*Sees Rames too.*) Rames, the great Priest! I understand. He would
steal you from me for his dismal Temple, steal you away from life.

Menophis

He is among the wisest and noblest of our land, the Great One of Vision, Aton's servant.

Nefertiti

(*Pouting, alarmed.*) Aton!

Menophis

Hush! Be careful! Even if Aton takes me, the chain of lives **must** bring us again together. It were but a brief separation—a sacrifice of pain and joy we both may offer as one being. And when, in our next life, we meet again, what ecstasy of strengthened, purified love would be ours—to know each had been faithful to the other—for His sake.

Nefertiti

(*Roused.*) Me grow old in loneliness while you satisfy your soul with selfish worship! *Our* sacrifice!

Menophis

In dreams we still—

Nefertiti

We should never meet; a dream's a dream. No children would come to me.

Menophis

You would not pine. It would be, for both of us, a preparation for our meeting in a future life—

Nefertiti

(*Playing on his feelings.*) You are right, Menophis. I should not pine, for I should marry and know joy. Your sacrifice, if you choose it, you may bear alone, for Nefertiti will not certainly be lonely. There is no lack of those who offer life to her in place of the dream that Rames sets before you—

Menophis

Others! Is there another? Nefertiti—! (*Approaches.*)

Nefertiti

(*Withdraws.*) Rames is coming. I hear his cautious step. Make your choice with him. I will not influence you. You wished to be alone; I'll leave you. (*Makes to move away.*)

Menophis

(*With passion and regret.*) One moment more. Will you not say farewell? And if—and if—until you hear from my own lips—

Nefertiti

(*Softly.*) If you decide to leave me, Menophis, you will not quite forget—

Menophis

Little Child, you know. Always I shall think of you—

Nefertiti

(*Mocking.*) As happy and light-hearted—with another. I am no "dream" to Sethos.

Menophis

Your beauty tortures me.

Nefertiti

You do not torture *me*; you cannot. If you loved me you could not give me up so lightly. You may think of me—of *us*—walking along this river bank at sunset with laughter and without regret, talking maybe of Menophis, and his passing dream. The echo of our laughter may reach into your little cell.

Menophis

(*Advancing.*) Unsay those haunting words.

Nefertiti

It is but impulse that betrays you. You have a "greater love" than me. I have one too! Farewell. I shall not come again unless you call me.

[*Exit.*

[MENOPHIS *paces to and fro, hides his face in his hands, sighs, looks after the girl, pauses, then bows his head and waits while RAMES comes up to him.*

Rames

Your eyes are troubled, although I cannot see them. (*Looks down at the young man's footsteps.*) And your steps leave an uneven pattern on the sands.

Menophis

(*Looking up.*) There are too many voices in my ears; and all are sweet. I know not which is true. I am unhappy and afraid. My peace of yesterday is gone.

Rames

These stars that watch you now shall watch your future lives as well. Before they pale at dawn they shall have marked your choice. They are rising in the east. They watch you—and they wait.

Menophis

(*Turning his look away from the sky.*) I came here to find peace—between the sunset and the sunrise.

Rames

Sunrise and sunset—the two great moments of the day. Death and resurrection—the two great moments of our life. (*Watches him closely.*)

Menophis

Not death—a disappearance only (*smiles*) for a little time.

Rames

(*Pleased.*) To return again and again, each new life linked to those that went before; and each determined by opportunities left or taken.

Menophis

The choice! Oh, Rames, there are two calls in me. I hear two voices always. My future life hangs upon the decision that I make.

Rames

You will not make it. It will make itself. The stronger call must win (*points across the Nile towards the sinking sun*). It is whether you shall live unto yourself alone, or consecrate your powers to Aton. (*Points towards the Temple.*) It is not alone your future life that hangs upon the choice; it is your future lives.

[*They spread their arms and bow towards the West. The sun sinks below the Libyan horizon of the desert. The dusk creeps up.*

Menophis

(*Rising.*) If only the whole of me could choose. I should then know that I am worthy.

Rames

(*Approving.*) There can be no half-heartedness in the service of our Deity.

Menophis

(*With enthusiasm.*) Our Deity—the sun!

[*Turns and gazes at the great Temple of Aton whose white columns still gleam in the golden after-glow some distance across the desert.*

Rames

(*Moving closer, with hand on his shoulder.*) Egypt, our great land, now witnesses the climax of her splendour. A change, which is divine, steals over her. It is no longer the mere disc of the sun we worship; it is the power behind.

Menophis

(*Reverently.*) The heat and glory that are in Aton, eternal and all-loving Deity.

Rames

(*Smiling.*) Who calls you for the offering of—yourself. (*Pauses.*) The Temples of our regenerated Egypt demand the best.

Menophis

(*Eagerly.*) And I might help towards this great uplifting?

Rames

(*Gravely.*) Menophis, Aton calls you to himself.

Menophis

(*Enthusiasm and awe on his face.*) I hear the call!

Rames

(*Slowly.*) But other, lesser, calls as well?

Menophis

There can be no turning back!

Rames

No turning back.

Menophis

I must be sure!

Rames

It is for ever.

Menophis

(*Very low.*) I know which call is highest, yet I hear that sweeter voice. If only I could smother it.

Rames

(*Understanding.*) It is the lust of life—of woman!

Menophis

It is love.

[*The dusk is turning into darkness. The stars begin to peep.*

Rames

I may not influence you. Years ago I heard these two calls, as you do, singing in my soul.

Menophis

(*Looking eagerly, with respect, into the old man's face.*) And you have never known regret?

Rames

(*Gravely.*) I have known perfect joy.

Menophis

To yield what is most dear to another is very hard. Oh, Rames, I am so young, the choice is difficult. If I had some sign that Aton accepts me—! (*With rising passion.*) Aton, guide my decision and grant my choice be wise!

[NEFERTITI *is seen returning.* SETHOS *is with her. They are laughing together.* SETHOS' *arm is about* NEFERTITI. *MENOPHIS does not see them.*

Rames

Weigh carefully. Hear every call with honesty. Aton, indeed, does call you, but it is all or nothing. (*Withdraws slowly down river bank towards the Temple. Waves his hand solemnly.*) I leave you—to yourself.

[*Exit.*

Menophis

Great Aton, guide me.

[*Stretches arms to the sky; looks up at stars. Then bows his head upon his hands in prayer.* NEFERTITI *draws near with* SETHOS.

Sethos

My head spins, Nefertiti. Then it was in play that you dismissed me? I can hardly believe my happiness is real.

[*Tries to embrace her.*

Nefertiti

(*Escaping gaily.*) Everything's real—at the moment when— you've got it.

[MENOPHIS *hears their voices. Turns and sees them.*

Menophis

With ... Sethos...! (*To her.*) You've come back...!

Nefertiti

(*Pretending she has just noticed him.*) The river bank is public, I believe. All Memphis will be here presently—this sacred night. (*Mocking.*) Forgive me—forgive *us*—if we disturbed your meditations. (*Glancing at Sethos.*) We enjoy the starlight like the other lovers!

Menophis

Together!

Sethos

A young girl does not come out unattended. I am proud that Nefertiti accepts my protection—as before.

Menophis

Little Child!

Nefertiti

(**To Sethos, laughing.**) Menophis, you know, is half a priest already. He has put aside all common things—youth, dancing, laughter—love.

Sethos

(**Half insolently.**) Wise Menophis! I envy a man grown old before his time. He has had some bitter disappointment probably.

Menophis

(**Suffering keenly.**) If you **really** love each other, I—

Sethos

Come this way, Nefertiti. I hear a pipe. (**Melody on pipe heard faintly.**) Let's go and dance. This atmosphere is too holy. (**Tries to draw her away.**)

Menophis

(**Pain.**) Can this be a sign from Aton—that you are worthless?

Nefertiti

(**Stung.**) We'll dance, yes, as we did at Memphis when the harvest ripened. And then we'll bathe together, Sethos. It all is worship, and my blood this sacred night is burning—

Sethos

(**Wild.**) And to-morrow I may see your father—?

[NEFERTITI *whispers in his ear. They laugh. He tries again to kiss her. She escapes again, and dances seductively, taking care to go close past* MENOPHIS, *who makes several half movements towards her, but controls himself.*

Nefertiti

(*Singing mischievously to the tune of the distant pipe, and holding Sethos by the hand. As she goes past Menophis she holds out her free hand to him temptingly.*)

"Come, dance together. Take my hand

Beside the rising river;

We'll dance upon the starlit sand,

And then through life—for ever!"

Menophis

(*Catching at her hand as she flits past.*) Nefertiti!

Nefertiti

(*Escaping his touch. Still hand in hand with Sethos.*) I heard a dead voice calling from a Tomb. (*To Sethos.*) It's not for us. *We* are alive!

[*Sings as before, glancing mockingly at* MENOPHIS, *who again would seize her as she goes by.*

"The rising river takes our feet,

And life flows full of laughter;

Come, dance with me while youth is sweet—"

Menophis

(*Touching her.*) Little Child!

Nefertiti

(*Slowing down. Sings last line lingeringly.*)

"The wedding follows after!"

Menophis

My Little Child.

Sethos

(***Trying to draw her away.***) Come, Nefertiti. Come with me, lest the Temple snatch you, too.

Menophis

Listen! The waters wait the sign! (***Warningly.***) A few brief moments and the Tear of Isis falls—and the choice is made, not for this life only, but for ever. (***Solemnly to Nefertiti.***) You would bind your soul to his … for all future lives … for ever?

Nefertiti

(***Drawing back.***) "For ever"! "For all future lives"! For an hour—a few hours, perhaps—

Sethos

You swore to me that you—

Nefertiti

I danced and played and sang with you. You dance lightly and your voice is sweet. But—if it is true that vows taken to-night can bind me to your soul for ever—

Menophis

It is true.

Nefertiti

… the journey would tire me.

Sethos

Nefertiti!

Menophis

(*Steps between them. Nefertiti hesitates.*) Let her alone. Since her eyes first opened to the sun she has been mine. A hundred future lives shall take our feet together. And she knows it. She plays with you—this singing, dancing. She *lives* with me. (*Seizes her, all else forgotten.*) Leave us together, Sethos. Go!

Nefertiti

I played with you. You know it. (*To Menophis.*) You had forgotten our appointment! I did it—for my love's sake.

[SETHOS *shrinks from his sudden violence, startled, but keeps her hand.*

Menophis

She has finished with you. Go!

Sethos

(*Sneers.*) Finished! You are mistaken, Menophis. Only a while ago she said my love was precious to her—(*Realising.*) You (*to her*) have strange ideas of play. You're a—

Menophis

(*Threateningly.*) Enough, Sethos. You knew, at least, that we belonged to one another. You have yourself to blame.

Nefertiti

(*Proud of him.*) Of course. Sethos says the same sweet things to many another maiden too.

Sethos

(*Bitterly.*) The Gods have set me free of you, and I am glad. When next we meet, Menophis, you shall hear the soft promises she made me (*turns his back to go*), and how she spoke of *you*! (*Moves faster, as Menophis advances threateningly.*) She called you half woman and half monk—no man at all (*runs*), fit ... only ... for ... the Temples!

[*Exit.*

Nefertiti

(*A last shot at him.*) Yet if I raised my little finger you'd come tumbling back—a helpless slave! (*Turns to Menophis.*) I am ashamed. (*Demurely.*) I did pretend he pleased me.

Menophis

Little Child....

Nefertiti

(*Happy.*) I was a little jealous of—of—your Aton.

Menophis

And I, perhaps, of your … Sethos.

[*They smile and embrace. The pipe is heard. She breaks away and dances before him happily.*

Nefertiti

(*sings*)

"Come, dance with me, and take my hand

Beside the rising river;

We'll dance upon the starlit sand,

And then through life—for ever."

Menophis

You are a daughter of the sun!

Nefertiti

Isis and Aton both are in our blood!

Menophis

Your beauty blinds me. I hear no other voice than your dear singing. I see no stars, your twinkling feet are everywhere.

Nefertiti

(*Triumphantly.*) It is the call of Life.

[A sound is heard, like wind in an Eolian harp, faint.

Menophis

(*Startled.*) Listen! The moment comes.

[With the sound is mingled the lapping of water.

Nefertiti

(*Awed.*) It is here.

[*A star falls from the sky.*

Both together

The Tear of Isis!

Menophis

Our river takes it.

Nefertiti

The waters rise.

Menophis

Our choice is made—for ever.

Nefertiti

My beloved. (*Embrace.*) Mine … for ever and ever … all our future lives.

Menophis

The Temple was a dream. Your beauty makes me see it. (*Breaks off as he sees Rames and Sethos approaching through the palms.*) Rames comes. (*Makes to hide.*) Great One of Visions!

Nefertiti

(*Triumphantly.*) And Sethos with him. Let them see us both. (*Catches his arm.*) Do not hide, but tell them boldly of your glorious choice.

[RAMES *and* SETHOS *have been talking together.* SETHOS *now turns and goes off towards the Temple, walking slowly with bowed head, but looking back over his shoulder sometimes. Disappears.* RAMES *comes slowly forward. Holds up his hands to bless them.*

Rames

(*Smiling gravely.*) May Aton bless you both—now—and in all lives to come.

Nefertiti

(*Confidently.*) Aton *has* blessed us—both.

Menophis

(*Dazed, troubled.*) Rames—you come to know my choice. (*Very gravely.*) The Tear has fallen. The river is rising, and I—(*lowers head*) I have heard the call.

Rames

The choice is yours—(*solemnly*) and *hers*.

Menophis. I have } chosen. The rising waters and the risen stars bear witness.

Nefertiti. He has

Rames

They … bear … witness.

Menophis

(*Half sadly to Rames.*) I have weighed both voices. Another—a worthier than I—must replace me in the Temple.

Rames

Aton does not compel. The call will come to you again—in following lives, until—

Nefertiti

(*Interrupting.*) Our love comes from Aton. He has given Menophis to me for my own.

Rames

All gifts are his.

Menophis

Holy Rames, I cannot let her go from me.

Rames

(*Solemnly.*) The choice is made. The future lives will bring again, and yet again (*turning to Nefertiti*), this same deep opportunity, when you—again—shall lead his soul higher, or (*with emphasis*) delay and hinder by vain selfish love.

Nefertiti

(*Defiant, yet frightened.*) He is mine—for ever. No priest or god shall rob me of him. I keep him for myself. (*Clutches him.*)

Rames

The rising water bears witness to your vow. (*With prophetic and intense gravity.*) Where the Temple gleams white in the sunlight, and where the palaces run down to the sea, you shall hear the waters in your soul—and—shall—remember.

Nefertiti

(*Alarmed.*) Listen! He prophesies!

Menophis

(*Awed.*) Great One of Visions!

CURTAIN

•••

ACT II
THEIR SECOND LIFE TOGETHER.
TIME—325 B.C.
GREECE

CHARACTERS

PHOCION (40), Athenian General.

LYDIA (35), his wife.

LYSANDER, a youth, PHOCION'S brother.

ALEXANDER THE GREAT

ATHENIAN CITIZENS.

•••

ACT II

SCENE—*Room in Phocion's house in Athens. Simple. Altar to Zeus with brazier burning. Colonnade with pillars and view towards Acropolis.*

Late evening.

(LYDIA *is half-kneeling, half-leaning over the marble balustrade, gazing into the distance. Enter* PHOCION. *He comes near and touches her.*)

Lydia

How you startled me!

Phocion

Were your thoughts so far away, Little Child?

Lydia

I was thinking.

Phocion

And gazing across the sea as usual. What is there so attractive beyond that dim horizon? The future or—?

Lydia

Perhaps its dimness only. That's southwards, is it not? There Egypt lies, and—Alexandria—you said—the great, new city.

Phocion

(*Searchingly.*) Distance still haunts your eyes. Little wonder that I startled you. (*Kisses her.*) But do not speak of Alexander's city. Our thoughts lie nearer home—in Athens.

Lydia

Where have you been, Phocion? All day I've missed you.

Phocion

On the hills—alone. I have been thinking.

Lydia

Thinking—you too!

Phocion

I came home by way of Theseus' Temple, saying a prayer for our loved city and for ourselves.

Lydia

But you are weary, and your feet are splashed with mud.

Phocion

I crossed the Ilissus to be sooner home, and found it rising—in flood almost. Yesterday's rains on Mount Hymettus—(*breaks off as she makes a sudden gesture*). Why, what ails you, Lydia? Do I startle you a second time?

Lydia

Forgive me, Phocion; do not notice my little weaknesses. It was merely—there, I've often told you—a rising river is an omen that causes me strange uneasiness.

Phocion

Little Child, I understand. I know your feelings. Athens herself is on edge these days—and little wonder.

Lydia

Phocion, let me tell you honestly—I am afraid.

Phocion

Anxious, perhaps, but not afraid. The mood of our beloved city takes you with it, as it takes us all. We all are patriots to-day. But the wife of Phocion has proved herself no coward.

Lydia

(*Low voice.*) Alexander is so powerful. Some say the Macedonian is a God.

Phocion

Pshaw! In his own land, perhaps. But Athens has her own Gods. He is a conqueror, yes; but a conqueror can only take a city, not the souls who dwell in it.

Lydia

(*Softly.*) Phocion, when I hear your words my fear melts away. Yet Athens *is* conquered. Our city trembles—

Phocion

Hush, Lydia. I do not like to hear you say such things.

Lydia

Who can stand against him, then? Who is there can oppose this conqueror of the Persians?

Phocion

Every Athenian—every Greek who loves our city more than he fears the Macedonian.

Lydia

All Athens, then!

Phocion

All the best in Athens.

[LYDIA *looks nervously over her shoulder towards the city and Acropolis. The dusk deepens. The first star shows.*

Lydia

(*Shudders.*) Your speech is often mysterious like this now—dark with meaning. Each night as twilight gathers from the sea about our city, there are footsteps on the causeway that make me tremble. No sooner has Hymettus darkened than shadows move silently over the courtyard and between the pillars. (*Turns and flings her arms about him.*) Oh, my Phocion, it is for you, not for myself, I am afraid.

Phocion

Calm yourself, beloved. I am an Athenian who obeys his unconquerable Gods. I do no more than accept the destiny they lay upon him who loves his country—

Lydia

But if Alexander discovered you—if—!

Phocion

Discovered me! What thought is this?

Lydia

If he discovered you were true to Athens, I was about to say. If he took you from me! Oh, Phocion! In dreams I have seen you lying dead at his feet—lost to me for ever.

Phocion

Not lost, most loving woman. If the Gods take me—if I die for Athens—

Lydia

Am I, then, less than Athens?

Phocion

Athens is great because of women like you, Lydia. You would not see her less?

Lydia

How less?

Phocion

Less free. Liberty is the breath of life.

Lydia

What is my liberty if I lose you? Your voice, your touch, your living presence here beside me (*embraces him*)—I want you alive and loving—

Phocion

Our love has grown with Athens. On the green Cephissian banks we first discovered it, and that evening on Hymettus when the honey—ah, I see it in your eyes, dear heart—you remember even as I remember. If Athens live—

Lydia

But if **you** die! If Alexander crush you, kill you! Oh, my Phocion, this struggle against the conqueror is vain. You tempt the Gods. I fear for you and for your hopeless schemes—

Phocion

My schemes! Lydia, what do you know?

Lydia

I suspect only. I feel you planning dangerous things that must take you from me. Those silent footsteps on our causeway in the dusk, the shadows that pass between the pillars, the rising waters—Phocion! your strange deep love of Athens takes no account of me, your little, suffering wife.

Phocion

The love of Athens is **ours**. It is the love of country that the Gods call sacred. (*Looks out across the fading city.*) Hellas, your valleys and mountains, streams and happy groves … beautiful, beloved … who would not die for you…!

Lydia

I love **you**. If you live for me, you live for Hellas even more. Athens lives in our hearts, not otherwise.

Phocion

(**Sternly.**) If a barbarian rule our dear city, our hearts are dead. It is better for my heart to mingle with the soil of Hellas than beat as the slave of Alexander.

Lydia

I love you too much to see you run on death. Your wild plot to save our city is but the Fates' way of taking you away from me.

Phocion

Try, Lydia, to love me as I love Athens.

Lydia

You ask too much of me. I love Hellas, but I love you more.

Phocion

Then—not enough. (**Looks away.**) You make it hard for me. I see the right so clearly, but your clinging love makes me weak.

Lydia

There is nothing in the world for a woman but her love. If you were lost to me, Phocion, these lips could kiss one other only—the rising flood (**shudders**) of our little Athenian river—or the sea.

Phocion

What comes, sweet wife, comes to both of us together. You are overwrought with sleeplessness and watching. Trust me and love me—more I cannot tell you now. Your love shall give me strength. (**He embraces her and moves slowly off towards the colonnade.**) And if there is a greater love than yours, some day we shall find it—know it both together. What comes to me to do now—I must do.

[*Goes slowly off.*

Lydia

(**At him.**) A greater love! Ah, Phocion—you're going from me—going towards death. I know not what you mean. There is no greater love. (**Watches him disappear.**) Then I must save you, since you will not save yourself. I cannot lose you. My love, I cannot let you—(**Covers her face with her hands**). My love shall save you from yourself. If I do wrong the Gods forgive—

[*Knocking is heard. She starts and looks round. A* MESSENGER *is seen in the courtyard.*

(**Cautiously.**) You would see—whom?

Messenger

The wife of Phocion.

Lydia

(*Frightened.*) Hush! Come softly, I am she. (*Messenger enters stealthily.*) You bring a message for me? You bring a token?

Messenger

(*With respect.*) She who sends me bids me say as token this: From one who loves her Lord more than his earthly glory—to her who loves as greatly.

Lydia

(*Faintly.*) To her who loves as greatly. (*Hesitates, shows agitation, a distraught expression on her face.*) It is to save him that I do it—to save his life for—both of us. (*Turns to Messenger.*) Your great mistress bid you bring an answer back to her?

Messenger

Without delay—my orders are.

Lydia

Have you no more to say? No further message? Do you bring only the token that you come from her?

Messenger

She bid me say that you should feel perfect confidence.

Lydia

The word of Alexander—?

Messenger

Has been given, and cannot change.

Lydia

Though it concern the life of one who was his enemy?

Messenger

The Queen bid me assure you. He has given her his promise. It will not alter.

Lydia

(*Whispers.*) Then take this message back to her who sent you: To one who comes hither to-night when the moon is high enough to cast a shadow I will reveal what I have promised to reveal. In return I claim the boon the conqueror has sworn—through her—to give me.

Messenger

Her word and his are both securely given. I take back yours.

Lydia

Go swiftly, silently. I shall await fulfilment here—when the moon is high enough to cast a shadow on the marble causeway. Behind that pillar I shall wait. Go swiftly!

[*Exit* MESSENGER. LYDIA, *looking anxiously at the sky, withdraws into the shadow of the pillars.* PHOCION *enters, his arm upon the shoulder of* LYSANDER, *his youthful brother.* LYDIA *overhears their talk.*

Lysander

(*With enthusiasm.*) Our last meeting now, and then to action. Oh, Phocion, I feel the Gods are with us. Your daring shall save Athens, and Hellas will live—even if we die.

Phocion

We all stand or fall together. They are picked men, and heroes; no one among them thinks of self. The risk, of course, is great, but it is nothing when the stake is considered.

Lysander

Everything favours us. The best troops of Alexander's army are still in Egypt. The entire city is behind us. All Athens will rise when it sees you are our leader. (*Vehemently.*) We shall drive the proud Macedonian out. Oh, I'm glad the talk is over soon! I burn for action.

Phocion

I, too, want action. I am not made for stealth and for conspiracy. Plotting and hesitation weary me. (*Sighs.*)

Lysander

Phocion, you feel no doubt, though——? I heard you sigh. Are you less sure of——of anything?

Phocion

For myself, boy, I have no doubt. For Athens I am sure and strong. Did I sigh perhaps? If so——if so, it was for others whose lives I hold in trust. For others——the truest, best, and bravest men in all Athens.

Lysander

The Gods will bear that burden for you, Phocion.

Phocion

Yes, yes; the Gods will bear it——partly.

Lysander

No one can lead but you. We are of one accord.

Phocion

I *will* lead, Lysander. Have no fear. Of myself I do not think. (*Looks out.*) The moon is up. I see the evening star o'er Salamis. They will be here very shortly.

Lysander

We are quite safe here. I took the password round myself at noon.

Phocion

We cannot be too cautious. Alexander's spies are more numerous than the bees upon Hymettus. They can sting as sharply too.

Lysander

Oh, our secret is well guarded. Yet the least whisper or thoughtless word could so easily betray us. (*Looks round with a moment's hesitation, then continues in a lower voice.*) I only would——that Lydia——

Phocion

Lydia!

Lysander

She is in great favour with Alexander's queen, Statira.

Phocion

So much the better! Since she knows nothing there is nothing she can reveal. Alexander seeks to play the generous conqueror. That the wife of Phocion accepts favours that Phocion spurns can only save us from suspicion. The Persian woman helps us without knowing it. And so does Lydia!

Lysander

You are right, Phocion. The Gods show their will in little things like this. We are under their protection. Yet if word reached Alexander of our gathering in your house to-night—

Phocion

Keep your words for later, boy; you waste your strength. How can you hold such idle thoughts? Hellas a Macedonian province! Her ancient liberties crushed! Our last hope dead as soon as born, and no blow struck!

Lysander

Phocion, forgive me! And, Selene, in yonder rising moon, forgive me too. The Gods protect and help us!

Phocion

Pallas Athena, give us wisdom to plan and strength to strike.

[LYDIA *comes forward from her hiding-place among the columns. The moonlight falls on her. As she moves she notices that it casts a shadow. She hurries.* LYSANDER *watches her somewhat closely.*

Ah, Lydia.

Lydia

You did not call me, Phocion? It seemed—

Phocion

(*Smiling.*) Your maidens called you to the bath. It is your bathing hour.

Lydia

(*To Lysander.*) Lysander, good-evening! You are fortunate. (*Half laughing, half jealous.*) Phocion has more time for his brother than for his wife.

Lysander

Had I a wife as brave and faithful as my brother has, I should be more fortunate still! These are grave times, good Lydia, for true Athenian men.

Phocion

Ah, Lydia knows too well, Lysander. But do not detain her now. (*To Lydia.*) I will come later for you, Little Child—an hour at the most.

Lydia

I am always ready for you, Phocion, and always true. I, too, am an Athenian.

Phocion

The Gods watch over you!

Lydia

And over you!

[PHOCION *moves to the balustrade and leans over, watching the night. He waits for her to go.* LYDIA *turns to* LYSANDER *and speaks low and hurriedly.*

You love him, I know, Lysander, and he loves you.

Lysander

Before he even knew your name, I loved Phocion, (*sternly*) and more than Phocion I love Phocion's honour.

Lydia

And so loving him you would urge him—to his death. (*With passion.*) You shall not, Lysander; Phocion is mine and he belongs to me. I will hold him fast to this life. A glorious career now lies at Phocion's feet.

Lysander

I love Phocion's honour too well to tempt him to dishonour.

Lydia

Tush, boy! You do not understand. I would not tempt him. Fate does not tempt, it commands. The high Gods bid us to accept fate bravely. The weak resist it; the strong accept and make it glorious. And a glorious career now lies at Phocion's feet.

Lysander

You speak with knowledge, Lydia? If so, how come you by such knowledge?

Lydia

Hush, not so loud. Lysander, you faithful brother, I tell you it is common knowledge. The Military Governorship of Alexandria—once offered to Phocion already and refused by him—is open to him still. Alexander knows his worth—

Lysander

His incorruptibility too. But how know **you** this, Lydia?

Lydia

I only know that Alexander is generous and will raise him to even greater honour. He places Phocion above all men in Athens—

Lysander

(*Coldly.*) Has Alexander's queen informed you thus. (*Louder.*) It seems strange to me, Lydia, that the wife of—an Athenian patriot—

Phocion

How loud your voices grow. Lydia, Little Child, you had best leave us now, for Lysander and I have grave business to transact together—and we expect others too.

[*There is a low knocking at the door.*

Lydia

Lysander chides me that I accept kindness from the queen of Athens' conqueror.

Phocion

I see no harm in that, and possibly much good. Your love will ever guide you. Farewell, now, for a little while. And happiness go with you!

Lydia

I leave you. It is your friends who come to you at twilight now so often. The Fates protect you, my Phocion! (*Whispers to Lysander as she goes.*) Oh, save him, Lysander! Save him from himself—for me, his wife!

[*Exit slowly, looking back fondly at* PHOCION *as she goes.* LYSANDER *watches her with an expression that betrays doubt, anxiety and disapproval. He shakes his head. The knocking is repeated. It is a definite knock that has been pre-arranged.*

Phocion

Open, Lysander. It is the Citizens.

[*A dozen* CITIZENS *enter quietly. Their leader holds a scroll in his hand. In turn they greet* PHOCION *with obvious respect, each giving the password, while* PHOCION *replies with the countersign:*

Citizen

The Gods deliver Athens!

Phocion

They will deliver her!

[*When all are in, they group themselves. An elderly* CITIZEN, *holding the scroll, acts as spokesman.*

It is safest our meeting should be brief, and no words wasted.

First Citizen

We stand for action.

Second Citizen

Immediate action.

Third Citizen

Each day that passes consolidates the barbarian power that would ruin Athens.

Lysander

Citizens, we need two conditions for success—to strike hard, and to surprise.

Phocion

We must move warily. The Macedonian's spies hide everywhere, and money has been flowing.

Lysander

There are ten thousand hearts in Athens above gold—!

Phocion

(*Gravely.*) Our preparations must be sure. You bring to-night the list of patriots?

First Citizen

It is drawn up (*holds out scroll*). Twenty names stand written here, each signed by his own hand, each guaranteeing three hundred men of arms—

Phocion

Whom we can trust?

First Citizen

The names are guarantee, as you will see—the best in Athens.

Second Citizen

Ready to live or die as our beloved city lives—or dies.

Lysander

And thousands more will follow once we show the way.

Phocion

Our forlorn hope (*takes the scroll*) is favoured of the Gods, and will be led by them.

[*Begins to read names.*

Citizen

Upon great leadership hangs success or failure. There can be one leader only.

Citizens

Phocion! Phocion!

Lysander

Phocion is our leader.

[PHOCION *reads silently.* LYSANDER *suddenly turns his head towards the moon-lit courtyard.*

(*Low.*) I saw a figure pass.

Citizen

A few moments ago I saw one too—between the pillars.

Another Citizen

Are we alone here?

Phocion

(*Looking up.*) My wife—and her maidens—are about. We are alone.

First Citizen

Once read, Phocion, the list must be instantly destroyed. Each signature is a warrant for the writer's death.

Lysander

(*Nervously.*) I counsel haste. The very stones move as with footsteps. The sky has eyes.

[*Turns towards a burning brazier close behind him.*

Phocion

(*Calmly.*) I have read. The names are—what Athens would expect.

Lysander

Then let me burn it.

First Citizen

(*Rising.*) Phocion, in the names you read, and in the names of all assembled here, we offer you the leadership—the military leadership. We ask you to lead our beloved city back to liberty again. (*Muffled applause.*)

[*While* PHOCION *has been reading, a woman's figure is seen creeping from pillar to pillar where the shadows are deepest. She is followed closely by a second figure—a man swathed in a head-dress such as that worn by the Persian warrior in the Elgin Marbles. Unnoticed in the dimness they reach the colonnades where they can hear all that passes.*

Phocion

(*Slowly.*) Citizens, in the name of Athens, and with the approval of the deathless Gods of Athens—I accept the leadership.

[*He hands the scroll to* LYSANDER, *who has stepped forward eagerly to seize it.* LYSANDER *turns towards the fire.*

First Citizen

Then we are half-way to success already. (**Applause.**) The sooner we disband, the better. Three of us may stay with Phocion to decide the final—

[*At this moment the cloaked figure steps out into the centre of the courtyard. He is plainly visible in the moonlight. Consternation reigns.* PHOCION *reaches for his sword.* LYSANDER *fumbles over the brazier, thrusting the scroll into the flames. The* CITIZENS *stand firm, not trying to hide, but visibly startled.*

Citizen

We are betrayed!

Citizen

A spy! We have been overheard!

Citizen

A Persian!

Phocion

(*Self-possessed.*) No stranger is unwelcome in my house, even though he enter—without permission. (*Louder to stranger.*) You would see Phocion? I am he.

[LYDIA *remains hidden in the shadows.*

Stranger

(*Advancing.*) I ask forgiveness for my unannounced intrusion. I disturb you. But my need is urgent. This is my warrant: I am a messenger from Alexander.

[*Stands erect and waits.*

Others

From Alexander!

Phocion

(*Calmly.*) You bring Phocion a message from Alexander?

Stranger

Of first importance.

Phocion

You may deliver it.

[LYSANDER *pauses to listen too.*

Stranger

A gift I am bid offer first—a gift from Egypt, where Phocion fought so bravely and so well. (*Holds out an object of gold.*) From the Temple of Ammon himself in Lybia.

Phocion

(*Coldly.*) Phocion fights not for gifts; nor can he accept anything from the barbarian conqueror of Athens.

Stranger

I am bid to urge reflection on you. First words are not the truest always, nor the wisest. (*Pauses.*)

Phocion

(*Simply, with scorn.*) I am an Athenian.

Stranger

(*Lays gift on a marble table beside Phocion.*) Alexander commands me say further—that, with this gift, he would honour Phocion by yet another one. He bids me call you the Military Governor of his new city in Egypt.

Phocion

The two gifts are one. I have one answer only.

Stranger

(*Smoothly.*) Then, with your answer, I ask permission to take back some trifle—such as that parchment the youth there would destroy—as proof to Alexander that the House of Phocion is loyal.

[LYSANDER, *startled, desists a moment.* PHOCION *takes a sudden step forwards.*

Phocion

(**Alarmed.**) Loyal——!

Stranger

(*Throws off disguise.*) The parchment.

[*Voice of command. Holds hand out.*

Phocion

Alexander!

[*All recognise* ALEXANDER. *Confusion, consternation, and murmurs:* "Alexander!" "Alexander!"

Alexander

Hand it to me, boy, before another name is burned. (*Laughs.*)

[ALEXANDER *strides towards him.* LYSANDER *defies him.* ALEXANDER *seizes him.*

He shall be surety, Phocion, for your loyalty.

[PHOCION, *holding his sword, rushes on* ALEXANDER *to aid* LYSANDER, *and above all to rescue the scroll. The* CITIZENS *stand their ground and are about to interfere, when* LYDIA *rushes in and throws herself on* PHOCION, *checking his violent attack. At the same moment* ALEXANDER *stamps on the marble floor.* SOLDIERS *enter.* PHOCION *and* ALEXANDER *stand facing one another in silence for a moment.*

I hold you the bravest man in Athens, Phocion, and such men as you I need. (*Holds out the scroll, as yet unread.*) But lesser men than you I do not—need!

Lydia

Phocion! Great Alexander!… Statira promised me…. Oh, he is too brave to die…!

Alexander

(*To Soldiers.*) Three of you take the boy away. The rest withdraw. No, let these greybeards go.

[*A few* CITIZENS *creep out, following* LYSANDER *and* SOLDIERS.

Lysander

(*Calling back to Phocion.*) The Gods will not desert us…!

Phocion

(*With dignity.*) You are the conqueror of Athens.

Alexander

Lesser men than you I do not need. Give me your allegiance (*pointing significantly to the scroll*) and I give you—these lives!

Lydia

(*Whispering.*) Phocion, you cannot sacrifice such men!

Citizen

Do not think of us! What is life to the conquered? Gladly would we die for Athens.

Alexander

I wait your decision, Phocion.

Phocion

(*Bitterly.*) Phocion, Military Governor of Alexandria, is Alexander's host.

Alexander

The word of Phocion is enough. (*Burns the scroll unread.*) Lysander, the boy, shall be Captain of your Bodyguard in Egypt. The Gods— your Gods—are witness to what I say.

[ALEXANDER *salutes* PHOCION *and goes out.* PHOCION *is alone with* LYDIA. *There is a moment's silence.*

Phocion

(*Brokenly.*) Athens! I have failed you! My life is broken in pieces.

[*Hides face in hands.*

Lydia

But I meant to save you, Phocion. My love would save you. Have I done wrong? Oh, tell me.

Phocion

(*Low.*) Youhavedone—your—best. Noone—nowoman—candomore.

Lydia

I could not face life without you. I could not see you die. My love made the desperate plan. I bargained with Alexander's queen—life with honour and glory for you in Egypt, the land you love. Oh, Phocion, beloved, do not judge me hardly. You do not speak.

Phocion

(*Patiently.*) There is something here I cannot understand.

[*His hand touches the gift from Egypt. He looks at it curiously, then looks out away from her.*

Lydia

I love you too much. Is that hard to understand?

Phocion

(*Sadly.*) Yet the love the Gods bring is otherwise ... I think.

CURTAIN

●●●

ACT III
THEIR THIRD LIFE TOGETHER.
TIME—FIFTEENTH CENTURY ITALY

CHARACTERS

PAULO SALVIATI, a painter, age about 25.

LUCIA, his wife, a beautiful Florentine.

PRINCE DAMIANO DI MEDICI, art patron.

•••

ACT III

SCENE—*Paulo's studio in Venice. A bare room of obvious poverty. Paulo painting at a large canvas.*

(Enter Lucia.)

Paulo

(**Turning happily.**) Lucia! At last you return. My love, how I have missed you. (**Kisses her.**) It seemed so long. (**Examining her.**) You are excited! Then my uneasiness was not for nothing. Tell me. An adventure, perhaps? An admirer, **of course**! This flush…! (**Laughs.**) Little Child…! (**Teasingly.**)

Lucia

I've been but a short hour, my Paulo. And, as for adventures and admirers, they have but one name—Paulo. (**Looks embarrassed slightly.**) How quick you are!

Paulo

Love makes me quick. I think I guess.

Lucia

(*Ashamed a little.*) Listen! (*They listen. The waves of the sea are audible beating against the outer walls.*) You hear?

Paulo

(**Patiently.**) I hear, but I do not understand. It is the water only——

Lucia

(**Lower.**) The rising water. (**Pauses, while passing hand over her forehead.**) Nor do *I* understand. It is my weakness, I suppose. All women have something that makes them fear without a reason, and this is mine——

Paulo

(**Protectively.**) For which I love you all the more. For had you reasoned you would not have married me. (**To himself.**) Strange, strange…. (**Recovers gaiety and turns to picture.**) See how it grows, Lucia. All that I scraped out yesterday I have repainted. Long before the Competition Day I shall have finished it. (**Enthusiastically.**) Look!

Lucia

The glow, the warmth, the colour—you've caught it all?

Paulo

I hope so. But when my model **and** my critic desert me both at once like this——

Lucia

Dear Paulo. (*Sighs.*) And it's so difficult for me to make five scudi do the work of ten. (*Shows agitation.*) I know, oh, I know. (*Excitement.*) Yet somehow, somehow we shall find a way. And it will be wonderful——

Paulo

(*Noticing her mood and wondering.*) It is you who are wonderful—(*shakes finger at her*) intriguing with Fate as ever——

Lucia

(*Quickly.*) No, not intriguing. I am but your wife—and model. (*Laughs.*)

Paulo

And inspiration——

Lucia

And critic——

Paulo

And manager! That is the wonder—that you who fled with a painter to learn poverty like this (**shows bare room**) and this (**shows** *clothes*) and this (***touches heart***) should bargain so cleverly in the market-place and carry home our fish and vegetables in your coloured apron—the Lady Lucia, a house-wife of the people!

Lucia

Forgetting the wine as usual, and dropping half the fish on my way! (***Seriously.***) Love makes it beautiful. It is for love's sake, Paulo.

Paulo

(***Emphatically.***) And the work's sake.

Lucia

(***Quickly.***) The work, ah yes, the work's sake. (***Excitedly.***) Oh, my Paulo, what would I not do—what would I not sacrifice for your advancement—I mean, for your art, your wonderful great art. (***Confused.***)

Paulo

(***Quietly.***) This shall be our love's first-fruits (***pointing to canvas***).

Lucia

(***Repeats low to herself.***) Our love's first-fruits.

Paulo

(***Rapt.***) When you and I float over the lagoons as dust upon the wind—(***turns to her from picture, and lowers voice***) when you and I are gone—remembered, perhaps, only as Paulo the painter, and Lucia his inspiration—this beauty—ah, that is my dream—this beauty shall still shine out for the world.

[*They watch the picture for a moment.*

Lucia

I fear one thing only for you—poverty. You should have ***everything***.

Paulo

I have. Everything that matters to an artist, and its name is inspiration.

[*Looks with passionate admiration at her.*

Lucia

(*With growing agitation.*) You left Florence for my sake. But for me, the great Princes—(*with an effort*) the Medici—would have helped.

Paulo

(*Brusquely.*) We agreed—(*pretended severity*)—solemnly, you remember— never to mention your princely lover's name. Nothing stops good painting like jealousy, and at *that* name I see blood.

Lucia

(*Smiling.*) Our Palace is too poor to house even that thin ghost. You have no need to think of jealousy.

Paulo

No need now, Lucia. In Venice we are safe from Damiano di Medici. Now, will you sit for me? I burn to work. Come! You must have roses in your hands. I will go to the flower-sellers by the bridge.

Lucia

I would have brought them with me from the market-place—one scudi each! I hesitated—

Paulo

And bought ten sprats instead! My wonderful, clever house-wife. Without sprats to eat I never could paint roses! But I must have them. I shall be but a moment away, my love—a single moment (*throwing kisses from the door*) that will seem like years! Farewell … Little Child.

Lucia

Little Child! Ah, how I love that name, given to me with our first kiss. I love it better than my own. (*Thinks a moment, puzzled.*) For somehow it seems my *very* own—

Paulo

It is your own. The little love-name that seems to travel like memory up the ages. I shall be back as soon as you are ready.

[Exit

[Knocking at the door startles her.

(Enter DAMIANO DI MEDICI.)

Lucia

You! And so soon. It is *too* soon. I've had no time to prepare him yet—

Medici

A painter receives his patron without preparation surely—

Lucia

Patron! You must not use that word to him, or all is ruined before it is even begun. You must remember—

Medici

(*Bows ironically.*) "Must" to me! And "must" again! My gracious Lady Lucia forgets—

Lucia

Nothing. She remembers that her husband, first of all, is proud, as I have already warned you. He does not yet know that I have been to see you—you, of all men in the world.

Medici

(*Frowning.*) When you say "proud" you mean, I take it, jealous.

Lucia

I mean both. (*Manner changing.*) Oh, Prince, you promised—I have your word that you would be guided in this by me.

Medici

(*Unbending.*) I was in haste to see the picture—

Lucia

But too great haste—

Medici

(*Ignoring her interruption.*) For he is, I swear truly, the man I need—his work, that is to say. (*Threateningly.*) As once, my Lady, you were the woman that I needed. But needs do not last for ever, nor is any indispensable—perhaps.

Lucia

(*More control.*) Oh, give me time, Prince, please. You do not want to lose him. I have your word and trust it. (*Anxiously.*) Will you not take your gondola to the islands—the sun is sweet upon the water—and return in half an hour? I—by that time I—

Medici

The light is sweet upon your face as well. What do you offer me in return for so great a favour?

Lucia

I am the wife of Paulo Salviati.

Medici

And have, as I see, married poverty as well as genius! I was too slow for once, as now, it seems, I am too hasty. I should have asked—and taken—all before this fellow—

Lucia

(*Scorn.*) Poverty with Salviati is beauty for *eternity*. The wealth of a Florentine princess belongs to *time*.

Medici

And, therefore, you come humbly to ask *me* a favour.

Lucia

One it should be an honour for you to grant (*with earnest persuasion*)—that you may share in giving eternal beauty to the world. Had I asked the Collona or the Calviere to see the work of a great painter whom poverty—

Medici

You came, instead, to me.

Lucia

You have bought the palace on the Grand Canal and need a great—the greatest—painter for your ceiling—

Medici

Enthusiasm becomes you. You look divine with that passion in your eyes.

Lucia

(*Cunningly.*) I am his model too, you see.

Medici

And that delicious gesture. (*Steps nearer.*) A little more fire, a touch more of abandon, and I swear that—on certain conditions—oh, very small ones!—I would grant everything you ask.

Lucia

(*Icily.*) An hour ago, when we talked together, you passed me your word. I appealed to you as lover of the beautiful—the best, the noblest in you. I was, it seems, mistaken, and our interview now had better end. (*Moves to window.*) I will call my husband.

Medici

This change from fire to ice is exquisite! (*Admiringly.*) But why so proud, fair Lady Lucia? (*She stands listening.*) You hear him coming? (*She hears the water lapping. Hides her face a moment.*) It is only the waves. The tide is rising still. That's all.

Lucia

(*Distraught.*) Yes, rising, rising. Please leave me, Prince. No, no—please stay—a moment longer. (*Frightened.*) Forgive me. Something—a vision-flashed upon me out of darkness. I am confused. I fear. (*To herself.*) Oh, I have done this very thing before—

Medici

But not with me, alas!

Lucia

(*Goes to his side.*) Forgive me. I thought only of myself. For a moment I forgot the work, the beauty that is his divine, his holy mission. Now I'm myself again. The water, the rising water—somehow—in some strange way—reminds me. Oh, I will be wise and loving in the noblest way. (*Looks into his eyes. Imploringly.*) It is his need, his poverty, that drive me to ask a favour of you who once aspired to be my lover. Have you no pity? We fled from Florence to escape you—it is true. I would rather ask favours of any in the world but you— (*Confused.*)

Medici

And yet—(*To himself.*) And you are his model. You could live for ever on my ceiling! (*To her.*) You are, indeed, a Goddess belonging to eternity! (*Admiringly.*)

Lucia

And yet—yes, I came to you an hour ago—as patron. It is true. It was for his sake and for his great art I came. (*Voice singing outside.*) Oh, I ask no favour now more than a little time to talk with him. That is his voice. I will persuade him. I will gain his consent, and he will do the picture for you—for your palace. Leave me, I beg, a few moments with him alone, and then return—to find—I promise it—the greatest painter in all Italy—

Medici

In all the world.

Lucia

Prepared to give you of his best.

[*Clasps her hands and stares into his face.*

Medici

To have you in my palace so (*admiringly*) is, perhaps, the next best thing to—have you in my—

Lucia

Oh, I implore you. Leave me with him. (*Singing comes very close.*) I promise.

Medici

(*Shrugging.*) You have chosen the one spell that moves me. Even more strong than the love of a fair woman is my love of art—its wonder, its beauty, and its triumph. His picture will outlive even your loveliness. (*Sighs.*) My name and my great palace will remind a later world of me, and of what I did for beauty. Well, well, my Lady Lucia, you win me over—for the moment, at any rate. I will stand behind this screen and listen. I must hear how you persuade genius to abjure its principles!

Lucia

(*Firmly.*) Then I do nothing. You must first go.

Medici

Another "must." Your self-will is adorable. Upon my word! But I, too, have a "must"—his work, with yourself as model, on my palace ceiling! (*Yields with a sarcastic bow.*)

[*Exit.*

[LUCIA *mounts the model's throne and stands, arranging her drapery, as* PAULO *enters.*

Paulo

(*Breathless; carries roses.*) Only two! They were so dear. I have not your skill in bargains. (*Holds out roses.*) We must make them do. (*Kisses her.*) Have I been very long? I had to go nearly to the Zucca.

Lucia

Two roses added to our love makes a whole garden. And one day soon you shall lack nothing the work needs. (*Tenderly.*) Oh, Paulo, beloved, by rights everything should be yours now. There is not a painter in Italy who comes near you.

Paulo

(*Quietly.*) I shall win the Competition. We shall have plenty then.

Lucia

(*Lower.*) Your art needs it *now*. (*Sighs.*) I am so useless to you—and yet—

Paulo

(*Looking.*) And yet—? Lucia, this anxiety, this nervousness is strange to you. You use unaccustomed words. "Useless"! What can you mean?

Lucia

You would never be angry—you would not scold me, no matter what I might do—for your work's sake?

Paulo

(*Passionately.*) You have such darling moods. I love you. The work is ours, not mine. (*Caresses her.*) I understand so well. It is your love that makes you tremble for the work's sake: the picture grows, the Competition Day comes nearer. It's like the sea-tides rising—it affects you—*I* understand!

Lucia

Yes, yes. You always know. You're always right. An inner tide seems rising in me as the time draws near. You understand my woman's moods, and so forgive them.

Paulo

(*Painting.*) Picture the scene, as we used to do when scudi were very scarce. It always makes us happy—the brilliant forecast.

Lucia

Tell me again. I love to hear it all.

Paulo

The judging will be in the Council Hall where the Doge holds high state, crowded with the noblest and loveliest of all Venice. The pictures chosen for the final verdict—that's Vernio's and Marco Gagliano's, and mine—I mean ours—of course—will stand apart on easels. And on a pillar in front of them shines the jewelled casket with the thousand gold pieces that Venice bestows—a mere trifle—upon him she decrees the greatest artist—

Lucia

And the pillar is garlanded with roses—more than these two, but not more lovely, Paulo.

Paulo

Of course. And the competitors waiting in a hungry, anxious group—

Lucia

You won't be hungry. I'll have so many sprats the night before—

Paulo

I shan't be anxious either.

Lucia

(*Happier.*) You will be dressed in a new doublet of purple cloth. If we can buy no golden thread for the embroidery I shall weave this across it. (*Holds out her hair.*) You'll look magnificent—

Paulo

The picture—

Lucia

Still more magnificent. They won't know which to look at—

Paulo

(*Merry.*) Then they'll squint.

Lucia

The judge will call aloud your name: Paulo Salviati. You will be victor, and all the Assembly will rise to honour you—

Paulo

(*Correcting her again.*) The work. My art, not me. My art, my work—

    [LUCIA *stands up to show the judge's gestures. She hears the water lapping. Her face changes.*

What is it, Little Child?

Lucia

N—nothing, Paulo. I—I merely thought a moment of those other painters, of Vernio, of Gagliano, the favoured ones who have wealthy patrons, so that they can work in ease and comfort, lacking nothing—

Paulo

(*Grandly.*) Except my inspiration—and my liberty. Think what that means. My work is done in freedom, and *must* surpass their best since it is bought of luxury. (*Earnest and contemptuous.*) What artist, no matter his genius, that can see truth while a patron jogs his brush, bidding him do this and that, set here a touch of gold and there of scarlet, put here a flower, a bird, and there a—a (*explodes*)—a sprat—! Why not? It is the soul alone that sees truth, and such men have sold their souls. They will be paid accordingly.

Lucia

(*Agitated.*) There are some patrons who—it is said—give freedom, liberty too.

Paulo

I never heard their names.

Lucia

There are some who know, who understand better. (*Confused and rapidly.*) They say the Medicis—

Paulo

(*Stops painting.*) Such painters and their patrons live for time, not for eternity, my Little Child. And among them the worst—the very worst—is that Florentine whose best claim to merit is that he dared to aspire to your love.

Lucia

I hate and despise him. Yet I dread his help—for others. He is as great in influence almost as his elder brother, Cosimo.

Paulo

Bah!

Lucia

Forgive me, Paulo—I reproach myself often that we fled from him—from Florence—where he might—(*lower*) oh, he *could* have done so much for you—his patronage.

Paulo

(**Staring.**) The mere name, as you see, stops me painting. You must not speak of it, here least of all in our place of work, of worship. Patronage—bah! My fire would go out, my inspiration leave me, my soul die in bondage. I must have (**loudly**) liberty.

Lucia

(**Frightened.**) The Madonna help me! Paulo, beloved, see what I have brought you—something your picture needs. My present and my surprise. No questions, now!

[*Holds out richly-coloured silk.*

Paulo

(*Delighted, amazed.*) That very broidery we saw together! Lucia—Little Child! How did you pay for it, or—or did you steal it? The merchant asked ten lira, I remember—and we had but three. (*Examines it.*) The colour of wine and pomegranate! Gorgeous! How did you pay for it? Quick, tell me. (*Lucia turns her head from side to side.*) The long gold earrings! Your last jewel! Lucia! (*Takes her in his arms.*) I'll kiss your ears (*softly*) till they leave blushes you cannot sell, fairer than any jewels, for they are the kisses of my soul which sees eternal beauty.

Lucia

Would that I had a whole casket of both kinds, my Paulo! Of one kind I would sell all. You should have a studio with north light, the best paints that can be bought, the choicest hangings, the fairest models, and—and, oh, everything these others possess who have not risked all for Love and brought a wife from Florence— (*Voice breaks and stops.*)

Paulo

Hush, hush, Little Child! You have given all you had—and that is everything. My art, if it is inspired as we dream, is stronger than circumstances, and will conquer. And I have liberty—love, beauty, liberty! What more can I ask of Heaven? Come, see the picture with me a moment. (*Draws her to it.*) Let us look at it together. (*They stand before it.*)

Lucia

(*Low.*) The Gods painted it.

Paulo

(*Moved.*) Your soul and mine, say rather. The hand is nothing. It is the inspiration. (*They look a moment.*) It was conceived, at least, in liberty—(*Starts and looks at her.*) You whispered something? I did not catch it. Tell me, Little Child. You feel—? Why, I declare, you tremble.

Lucia

(*Very low.*) One thing, I fear, one thing alone! The golden bloom, the warmth, the joyous laughter and the richness all Venetians love. It will be judged with the work of—of others whom plenty and comfort and—and all that help which money can provide—

Paulo

Men who feed from their patron's hands like obedient lap-dogs—

Lucia

Madonna, help me! They have never to calculate if their blue paint can last till the sky is finished. (*Impetuously.*) Why, in Florence, the Medici gives his painters—

Paulo

That name again!

Lucia

I chose it at random—by mistake. It slipped out, I mean. (*Losing control more.*) Oh, my too proud Paulo, if you only knew how I love your pride and worship it. I only thought—for a moment only— the merest foolish moment—that this young Medici—oh, he loves beauty too, he worships art and beauty—*perhaps*—I wondered—he *might* have helped in a way that even you could have accepted without losing your liberty. I reproach myself so—

Paulo

(*Sternly.*) Lucia, I need no man's help. I have told you. You doubt my art, my power, when you show this fear. It is fear that makes you reproach yourself. Our love knows no fear. (*Soothes her.*)

Lucia

It is, perhaps, myself I fear, Paulo. A strange dread haunts me like a dream. I fear lest I injure your great work, your mission—

Paulo

You tremble still. You are excited. Tell me, Little Child—do you know something that you hide from me—that you cannot tell me?

    [*Pause.*

Lucia

Nothing, nothing, but my woman's mood. My passion to help you is so great I sometimes fear lest I guide it wrongly—(*breaks off*). See, Paulo, the light is good, and we have this broidery you need (*replaces old drapery with the new silk piece*)—the very thing—exactly the tint and texture. I'll sit for you. (*Shows hurry.*) There is no time to lose. Some one might disturb us.

Paulo

(*A look of suspicion comes and goes. He watches her puzzled, while mixing his paints.*) Your mood is *new*. That is what disquiets me. You seem expectant almost. And this strange haste, Lucia? We never hurry!

Lucia

(*Laughing gaily.*) Only that I long to see this colour (*touches silk*) in your picture—on the very canvas, alive and burning—before it is seen by—by others.

Paulo

(*Absorbed.*) Yet who should see it before the Competition Day?

Lucia

Of course, of course. Still I am anxious. Time is precious. (*Poses.*) Oh, how lovely the silk lies on me! Look! And am *I* right? (*Whispers.*) Paulo, I feel your brushes on my heart. Paint swiftly, beloved, swiftly.

Paulo

Beautiful! Perfect! Divine! There—just as you are now. Don't move! Even your heart must stop!

Lucia

Madonna, help me!

Paulo

She does. Have no fear for the result. (*Paints hard.*) Now, talk to me while I work—no movement, mind! Just words. I love the music of your voice. It soothes and blesses me. The gossip of the market-place, for instance?

Lucia

(*Quickly.*) Ah, well, then the Eros will interest you—the one we coveted so…. It's gone from the merchant's booth at last.

Paulo

Our Grecian Eros! Our little statue! I shall miss it. I wonder who bought it. Or has it flown back to Samos, starved with yearning, on our summer wind? Some day we'll follow it. Greece! Glorious mother of artists! My heart lies there—sometimes, I almost think, my memory too. (*Pause.*) Who bought our Eros? Did you hear that as well?

Lucia

The critics say that in your art Greece has come back to life again.

Paulo

Who bought it, Lucia? Your head to the right a little—so.

Lucia

A great Prince, a stranger to Venice, they said, who has bought the Cavaliere Palazzo on the Grand Canal. Gossip is full of it. He has sworn to make it more beautiful than Cosimo Medici's in Florence—

Paulo

That odious name again! (*Smiling.*) It haunts you, Little Child! (**She starts.**) Don't move! don't move! The pose is perfect.

Lucia

Haunts the gossip of the town, rather—for which you asked me, Signor! The ceilings are to be painted with classical scenes alone—the loves of Apollo, and Athena's triumph.

Paulo

What subjects! And I know that Palazzo. Its ceilings are superb, enormous! Painting the very sky! (*Steps back to examine his work.*) It's coming, it's coming, the very colour I wanted. Yes, yes, they are the biggest in all Venice, so I'm told. (*Turns to her.*) Now, just suppose, Lucia—just suppose that one day——

Lucia

(*Nervous.*) Paulo, beloved, do not stop. Paint on quickly. You are in your best vein. Paint on before—before the light changes. Yes, and I heard one other thing.

Paulo

(*Painting.*) Ah!

Lucia

That this Prince will commission the winner of the Competition——

Paulo

(*Looking up.*) To paint those ceilings! Not unlikely, Lucia! There are menial fellows enough with talent who would do it. *I*—win or lose—*I* accept no commission tainted by patronage. And I *shall* win. What was this Prince's name?

Lucia

(*Excited.*) And those ceilings might be yours!

Paulo

Who is he?

Lucia

S—some said one thing, some another. I——

Paulo

The merchant must have delivered his Eros—to somebody—somewhere.

    [*Watches her.*

Lucia

He didn't say. I didn't ask **him**. It was the gondolier as I came home. Oh, Paulo, I cannot sit well for you if you cross-question me like this! You're like a judge. I love you so. Why should you suspect——?

[*Rises agitated.*

Paulo

Suspect! *You!* Clear water cannot hide the reflections in it. (*Expression of comprehension dawns on his face.*) Even if your love guided you amiss, I—I could never think, and far less use—that ugly word! Lucia! Little Child! You tremble—— (*Starts forward.*)

[*Enter* OLD WOMAN, *flustered.* LUCIA'S *hand flies to her heart.*

Woman

Signor! Signora! A great gentleman comes for you. His gondola is already at the steps. I heard him give orders to wait. I ran on to warn you.

Lucia

(*Cry.*) Already!

Paulo

(*Half incredulous still.*) Great gentleman! (*Looking at Lucia.*) Asking for—us!

[LUCIA *silent, face in hands.*

Woman

He is no Venetian. By his liveries he must be a Prince at least, and a great one. Your dress, Signora! (*Arranges it.*) He's come to buy the Signor's pictures! Your fortune's made. Oh, happy day! *I* will open the gate for him, so he will not know you have no servant.

[*Exit.*

Paulo

(*Grim.*) I do not understand. (*Makes to fasten door, hesitates, then turns to Lucia.*) *You* can explain this to me—Little Child—perhaps?

Lucia

Paulo, Paulo, do not be angry. Oh, forgive me, I implore. For your dear sake—for your work, your art—for you, I did it. It is not **me** he comes to see. It is your work, your picture. I went this very day—but an hour ago—to make him come. Oh, tell me, tell me I have not done wrong!

(OLD WOMAN *opens door. Enter* MEDICI.)

Paulo

(*Aghast.*) Damiano di Medici! Here!

Lucia

(*Hand on his arm.*) Paulo! Paulo!

Medici

At your service, Signor Salviati. (*To Lucia.*) Signora bellissima! Am I too early still? My promise—you remember—I was impatient to fulfil it.

Paulo

Promise! What can a Prince of the Medici promise to my wife?

Medici

(*Gravely.*) That which only the proudest painter may receive gladly from a humble prince: appreciation of his work.

Paulo

(*Coldly.*) My work is not done for the appreciation of princes. I have no work to show.

Medici

Your wife, Signor, said otherwise. And she is a rare judge of values. (*Bows.*) A faultless critic! (*Bows to her.*)

Paulo

The Prince di Medici knows.

Lucia

(*To Paulo.*) Oh, do not anger him. And think a little of *me*. You forget the risk—for your sake—that I ran—(*imploring*) your career——

Paulo

(*Watches her thoughtfully, weighing things that perplex him.*) Love led you a strange errand.

Lucia

For the work's sake, my Paulo.

Medici

The Medici have short memories for their failures. (*Laughs.*) Her courage—in coming to visit me—was even more rare than her (*glances at the picture*)—her judgment.

Paulo

(*With effort.*) She went to see you—yes. It was a mistaken courage that earned you a favour of that kind.

Medici

(*Suave.*) Even in Venice a Medici does not receive strangers—without a name—or, shall I say, whose name is yet to win. Your wife, Signor, had the courage to get her way to me past half a hundred lacqueys. But more! She had the eloquence and wit to persuade my return visit—here. She assured me your picture was worthy of my personal, my immediate inspection.

[*Goes to it.* PAULO *starts forward to prevent him.*

Lucia

(*Catches his arm.*) Paulo, beloved—by our love, by little Eros (*frantic*), by everything!

[MEDICI *moves the picture into better light.*

Medici

(*Watching them out of corner of his eye.*) With your permission. (*Bows.*) You will, perhaps, forgive the liberty. The light fails suddenly a little. So—(*examines critically, with signs of pleasure*).

Paulo

(*Back turned.*) For your sake, Little Child, I endure this cruelty.

Lucia

I yearned to help——

Paulo

So it was he who bought the Eros too? (*To himself.*) This is an evil
omen. (*To her.*) I thought us safe in Venice.

Lucia

You are so calm, so quiet. You terrify. I would fear your anger
less. Oh, my great Paulo, my dear, listen to me one moment. This
family—this man—vile though he be—loves art and beauty, and in so
far is not—Oh, I mean—oh, Paulo, it is his ceilings, his palace, his
help to your career that have betrayed me! You could bring Greece to
life in Venice—and for ever. Think not of him. Think only of your
beauty—lighting the world when he is dust——

Paulo

(*Quietly.*) Is my art so poor a thing—have you so misunderstood
it—that you think it is for sale?

Lucia

(*Distraught.*) Have I done *that*!

    [MEDICI *turns from the picture to* PAULO.

Medici

(*With reverence.*) You have been taught of the Gods—the Gods of Greece.

Paulo

(*Frigidly.*) Your praise——

Lucia

Hush, oh, I beg you—for *my* sake.

Medici

The drawing is the equal of del Sarto's and the composition no
poorer than da Vinci's. I swear it. Yet—the colour—hmm—I miss
Titian's glory. Those shadows (*pointing*) are out of tone a little——

Lucia

(*Quickly.*) We ran out of blue that day, alas———

Medici

Your model was, certainly, perfect. But why have you painted the nymphs from her as well as their divine mistress?

Lucia

Models demand impossible prices———

[PAULO *puts his hand on her mouth angrily.*

Medici

(*Reflecting.*) So little more, and it were a masterpiece. Even now it should win the Competition, by rights. Yet Vernio's is just a shade more rich, more splendid. I have seen it. And Gagliano has a purer colour. But then, of course, Gagliano buys his paint from that fellow by the Zucca who has a secret method—and charges accordingly, the scoundrel!

Paulo

(*Unable to contain himself longer.*) I paint as I desire, and as I can. The picture is mine. And not for sale!

Medici

(*Kindly.*) I admire your spirit, Signor. It has the independence of ancient Greece herself. Yet at what price? You may be satisfied with yourself, but your art thereby suffers. It becomes a slave of your conditions—if you will allow the language.

Lucia

Oh, it must be so! Paulo, it must be so! You see?

Paulo

(*Proudly.*) Conditions that leave the spirit free, at least. The spirit of beauty owns no master———

Medici

The husband of such beauty should be more gracious. (*Frankly.*) Ah, Salviati, you speak to a Medici, indeed, but also to one who loves beauty as you yourself do. I might—had I persisted—have taken your golden bird in my own net. (*Pauses.*) It is my pleasure now to set you free from the hard conditions that enslave you. In this way can a Medici reward good for evil. Signor, I forgive all for the sake of your genius. I admire your picture—its true classic spirit. Yet it has not quite the warmth, the fire, the bounteous splendour we Italians ask. Give but your sky a deeper hue, add to that robe the undertone of scarlet it needs to make it felt, flood our prodigal Italian sunshine over it all—and I will buy your picture at your price.

Lucia

Yes, yes. Oh, Paulo, what an offer! Think!

Paulo

It is not for sale.

Medici

While you may still enter it for the Competition. The judges—er—may hear that Damiano di Medici has bought it for his new Palazzo—and—judge—accordingly.

Paulo

(*Low.*) The gold, the blue, the scarlet you desire—I mean, suggest—are not in my scheme.

Medici

Yet they would add the perfect touch now lacking—in my judgment, Signor. Come, now, I will go further. I have sworn that my Palazzo shall surpass even that of Cosimo, my ambitious brother, in Florence. I will have a Gorgione for his Lippo Lippi, and—if you will—a Salviati for his da Vinci. I offer you, further, the painting of my ceilings, Signor—seven years' inspired and happy labour.

Paulo

Seven years of bondage to another's taste and purse.

Lucia

(*To Paulo.*) You could do your own work too.

[*Looking at* MEDICI.

Medici

Why not?

Paulo

To add this gold and blue and scarlet is—for me—a lie.

Lucia

Oh, my beloved, think, think a little, and weigh your words!

Medici

My offer stands—but not against unreasonable resistance. I repeat it: this picture at your figure, and seven years to paint the ceilings, with a certain freedom in design and subject, and permission to do your own work in your leisure. It is a matter to conclude now quickly. (*Ominously.*) It is not amusing, though it may be novel, for a Medici to be thwarted of his will—his deep design. (*Bows.*)

Paulo

A poor painter dares the novelty.

Lucia

(*Cries.*) You forget everything, Paulo—me you forget even—when you say such words!

Medici

(*Impatient, half-threatening.*) Beauty has turned your head, maybe. Excess, I have heard it said, (*significantly*) can affect the reason. You have (*glancing towards Lucia*) *too* much beauty. But there are remedies——

Paulo

(*Startled.*) I do not understand you.

Medici

As a great patron, I have my duties too. (*Slowly.*) If the possession of too much beauty threaten your great gift, I owe it to the world to (*sinister tone and look*) help—to save you.

Paulo

(*Facing him.*) I prefer plain spoken language from a man—even though he be patron.

Lucia

Oh, guard your tongue at least! The Prince is patient with us.

Medici

(*Softly.*) You robbed me once of beauty I desired. You fled from Florence. I accepted with a smile, and did not bestir myself to follow and prevent—as I could well have done. I was too kind, perhaps———

Lucia

(*Breaks in.*) But, great Prince, you—you have forgotten all that. You swore———

Medici

(*To her.*) The sight of beauty stirs my memory again. (*Suggestively.*) For beauty grows, it seems. (*Smiles admiringly.*)

[*He moves a little towards her.* PAULO, *with clenched hands, is held back by* LUCIA.

Lucia

(*To Medici.*) My Lord! (*To Paulo.*) Oh, Paulo, hold yourself! Am I so little to you?

Medici

And this increase of beauty makes me remember something I had—(*to Lucia*) as you say—forgotten. To see him who robbed me become my dependant—would have the true Grecian touch of comedy. (*Turns abruptly to Paulo with changed tone.*) Salviati—before the light fails, will you now dip your brush in the gold and scarlet *we* suggested?

Paulo

Never! Even in fading light I see only truth.

Lucia

Ah! Oh!

Medici

(*Looking from one to the other, then to the picture.*) There are many flowers in my gardens, but Italy holds one Salviati only. (*Reflects.*) My ceilings need him. I swore, besides, to Cosimo——

Lucia

(*Distraught.*) My Lord, my Lord, you promised——!

Medici

(*Brusquely.*) That I would see the work and offer my patronage—if it pleased me. That offer still holds good. But your husband is obstinate——

Paulo

I am true. I claim only liberty.

Medici

(*Darkly.*) So I must remember my duties as a patron—and apply remedies that may save his unreason—and his—art.

Lucia

(*Alarmed.*) What can you mean——?

[MEDICI *claps his hands.*

Medici

Ho! Ho! Without there! (*Four Men in livery rush in.*) Take the woman, but do not hurt her.

[MEN *seize her.*

Lucia

(*Struggling.*) Ah, Dios! Madonna, help me! Alive—never! Paulo! Paulo!

Paulo

(*Tries to fight his way to her.*) Never while I live either.

[*Draws a dagger.*

Medici

(*To Men.*) Disarm him—gently, gently. No injury. Who bruises that right hand of his answers with his life, remember! Strike up the dagger instantly.

Men

(*Struggling.*) For a painter he fights well.

Careful there! His hand—your sword's point!

His right hand, yes. Be wary.

This is rare sport.

Have you got the arm? Hold fast.

I've got the dagger.

He's safe, my Lord.

[*They hold him, disarmed.*

Lucia

(*Held.*) Paulo, my Paulo! (*Moans.*) Oh, that I were dead, to have done this thing!

Paulo

(*Firmly.*) My soul stands by yours. I know you true. Fear nothing!

Medici

(*Quietly.*) Signor Salviati, I regret that my sense of duty—my deep desire that you shall achieve your greatest—force me to this unpleasant remedy. But poverty is not helpful to your work, and I must—as patron of unreasonable genius—protect your art and yourself. I offer, therefore, the best help in my power. If you accept—then I need take nothing (*glancing at Lucia*) from your store of beauty.

Paulo

Dios! This cruelty—this treachery!

Lucia

No, no, no. Paulo, do not think of *me*———

Paulo

It is too late. (*To Medici, with effort.*) Your vile scheme means this, then: that I submit my art to your paid dictation, become your creature, or you will—(*struggles violently*). Let me free! (*to Men*). This bastard is not fit to live.

A Man

Hush! He is a Medici—Cosimo's own brother.

Medici

My gondola waits. My new Palazzo lies but half an hour distant—ready to welcome its first fair ornament.

Paulo

(*Wild.*) To be broken and thrown away when done with! Death is better now.

[*Tries to injure his right hand against a sword.*

Medici

(*To Men.*) Careful. Hold him. Or your lives———

Lucia

(*Frantic.*) Beloved, it is *not* too late. Forget that I live—oh, forget me—for your work's sake! Remember beauty only———

Paulo

(*Tender patience.*) Little Child! My work and beauty live with liberty. (*Very softly.*) Had you forgotten? Did belief in me waver, or did love guide you strangely—misconceiving———?

Medici

(*Impatient.*) The light fails rapidly. The gold and scarlet should be laid on now, before dusk falls. (*To Men.*) One of you go and prepare my gondola—for a lady. (*Man goes to door.*) Lay a soft silken scarf upon the cushion—there must be no screams in Venice. (*To Paulo.*) Oh, I will do it gently, Signor, with my own two hands. There shall be no roughness, no unkindness. (*Man gives scarf.*) Oh, here is the very thing. (*Goes towards Lucia.*) You will take this small attention from me, I beg, if nothing else.

Lucia

I hate you! Your touch is poison.

    [*Struggles.*

Medici

You should not ask favours, then, of those who poison you. (*Puts scarf round her arms.*) For the mouth I have a yet softer silk, as you shall see. Ah, the Medici, they say, are fortunate in love, and I shall find a way to win you. These arms I am forced to bind shall yet twine willingly about my neck———

Paulo

(*Shouts.*) All I possess to him who kills him!

Medici

All you possess!

Paulo

(*Yields.*) And more—my liberty. Let her go!

Medici

So reason returns, at last. The remedy works already towards a cure.

Paulo

Set her free. I give my word.

Medici

Though I trust no man, I trust **your** word, Salviati.

Paulo

(*Stammering.*) Unfasten me. Give me my palette.

Medici

(*To Men.*) Release him. Release the lady too. But watch him closely, lest he hide a weapon.

Paulo

(*Free.*) This is my only weapon (*takes brushes, etc.*). With it I put chains upon my soul. So—and so.

[*Dabs on paint.* LUCIA silent. Collapses to her knees and hides her face.

Medici

Improved already! So swiftly! You are, indeed, the greatest of them all. We shall beat Verio out of court, and Gagliano will die of envy on the spot. (*To Men.*) Begone with you! No, stay a moment—take the picture with you and lay it carefully in the gondola. It shall be finished under my own eye—before the ceilings are begun. (*Men obey.*) Carefully! One smear and your lives are forfeit. (*Turns to Lucia and raises her.*) You are not quick to thank me, Signora, yet I have fulfilled my promise to you. All that you begged of me is accomplished. Henceforth Salviati, your husband, shall work in comfort and lack nothing.

Lucia

(*Faint.*) How—how could I have done this thing? What ancient deep perversity—what lack of faith—what hidden destiny in me? (*To Paulo.*) Paulo, look, look at me! (*He keeps his back to her. Medici watches them quietly.*) Hark!

[*Sound of water lapping heard outside.*

Medici

So you will not thank me—either one of you? No matter. I like a little spirit. (*Goes to door.*) Carefully, now! The edges safe. No flick of dust, mind.

[*Stands looking down steps.*

Lucia

(*Low.*) Hark! (*To Paulo.*) It is another sound I hear. (*Whispers.*) Paulo! It is water. (*Stands listening intently to the lap of the sea. Distress increases. Passes hand over forehead, as if trying to remember something.*) The rising water! (*She turns her head slowly to look at Paulo. He turns slowly too. Their eyes meet. Very low.*) You hear? (*Whispers.*) That sound is in my soul. Paulo—I half remember—something—that hides behind it, yet comes with it. (*Goes up and clings to him.*) I have done this thing before—destroyed you—with my selfish love.

Paulo

Hush, hush!

Lucia

You look so strangely at me. Your face changes. Dios! (*Frantic.*) Speak to me, beloved! If you cannot forgive—say that you understand. Oh, what is it in your eyes? (*Fear.*)

[*Dusk increases.*

Paulo

(*Tender whisper.*) The night is coming—with her stars. In my eyes is only love. (*Patiently.*) There is nothing to forgive. (*Embraces her for several moments. Then breaks suddenly away.*) Where is the gold—the scarlet? (*Bewildered. To Medici.*) What is my Lord's desire?

Lucia

(*Screams.*) Oh, I have killed—killed *again.*

[*Falls.*

Paulo

(*Catching her.*) Little Child!

Medici

(*Turning at the scream.*) She is even more beautiful than I first thought. Well, well, the picture is mine at any rate, and she—(*smiles*) A good evening's work. How dark it grows. And the rising tide is at the full. Ho! Without there! My gondola!

[*Exit.*

[PAULO and LUCIA in each other's arms.

CURTAIN

•••

EPILOGUE
PRESENT DAY

CHARACTERS

PHILLIP LATTIN.

MRS. LATTIN.

THE DOCTOR.

EPILOGUE

SCENE—SAME AS PROLOGUE.

TIME—PRESENT.

(Mrs. Lattin opens her eyes slowly. The Doctor, near the bed, is seen making a gesture with his arms as if lowering a curtain. Mrs. Lattin shows bewilderment.)

Mrs. Lattin

(Dreamily.) Where am I? Florence ... Greece ... Egypt ... where are they? I am back again. But *who* am I?

Doctor

You are your Past.

Mrs. Lattin

I slept? But yet I lived it. I understand at last. I have found life.

Doctor

You cannot die, nor can *you* sleep.

Mrs. Lattin

But time....

Doctor

Is the body's measuring.

[*She looks round the room, and finally into his face. He moves slowly backwards towards the door.*

Mrs. Lattin

(*Thinking.*) It was not a dream. I was in Greece with Phocion ... with Paulo in Italy ... with.... Oh, it is too long ago, too far away. It's fading. (*Eagerly.*) Oh, I would not forget!

Doctor

The results lie in you. That is memory.

Mrs. Lattin

Each time I injured ... thwarted the highest in him by my selfish love. How small my love! Oh, tell me it is not now too late....

Doctor

(*By door.*) There is no "too late." What he could do without was added to him. You have taught Menophis, Phocion and Paulo to become ... Phillip.

[*He begins to fade.*

Mrs. Lattin

(*Joyfully.*) I understand at last, and I am healed. I delayed Menophis. I shall inspire Phillip. I shall go with him ... back to ... Egypt. Phocion, Paulo, how happy *they* will be!

Doctor

(*Almost invisible.*) He is coming now. I leave you.

Mrs. Lattin

But *he* must see you too....

Doctor

(*Invisible, only a voice heard.*) He cannot.

[*Door opens.* PHILLIP *enters quietly. He shows surprise at finding her sitting up. Her hands are stretched out towards the door where the* DOCTOR *has vanished. As he enters, the clock strikes the last three strokes of six o'clock.*

Phillip

You rang. I just slipped back to see——

Mrs. Lattin

(*Low.*) Phocion … my faithful.…

Phillip

Eh? Are you all right? I mustn't stay. Doctor Ogilvie will be here any minute.

Mrs. Lattin

(*Low.*) Paulo … my dear one.… I——

Phillip

(*Puzzled.*) You slept a moment probably. Good! (*Startled by her happy expression.*) You look … so much better!

Mrs. Lattin

He came. And I am healed.

[NURSE *enters hurriedly.*

Nurse

(*Whispering to Phillip so that Mrs. Lattin does not hear.*) Dr. Ogilvie has just telephoned. He is detained. He cannot get here till seven o'clock.

Phillip

All right. Hush!

[*Exit* NURSE.

Mrs. Lattin

He told me … showed me … everything.

Phillip

(*Humouring her.*) He gave you hope—the best? I see it in your eyes.

Mrs. Lattin

It's not—*I* am not—too late. That's all.

Phillip

Hush! Hush! Lie quiet a little longer. (*Goes on to ask, still humouring her.*) You mean the doctor says———?

Mrs. Lattin

I am so happy. I know and understand now. It's glorious.

Phillip

My darling! Gently, gently! Do not excite yourself. Lie still and sleep, if you can, again. He has given you something? Later, you shall tell me———

Mrs. Lattin

Ah, your great patient strength! It is too wonderful. And to think that my weakness helped, my selfish———!

[*Sits up and peers closely at him, shading her eyes with one hand.*

Phillip

(*Anxious, puzzled.*) The lamp is in your eyes. I'll move it. Do not stir. There, is that better?

Mrs. Lattin

Thank you, but I do not mind the light. I mind nothing. Thank you (*the name comes back suddenly*), Phillip. Ah, it *is* Phillip! I know you again—as you are—to-day!

[*Passes hand over forehead. Sighs and leans back. But face happy and at peace.*

Phillip

Mary!

Mrs. Lattin

Not Mary: Little Child.

Phillip

My—Little Child. (*Doubting and perplexed.*)

Mrs. Lattin

Phillip, dear heart, I've seen—I've seen my past—with you.

Phillip

(*Soothingly.*) Yes, yes. When you're more rested you shall tell me everything. Your dreams———

Mrs. Lattin

I must speak now. I've seen **our** past.

Phillip

(*Bewildered.*) Tell me, then, dearest, tell me. Then you must lie still———

Mrs. Lattin

(*Firmly.*) Life!

Phillip

(*Impressed.*) Life!

Mrs. Lattin

I have recovered. I love you more—but differently. I can forgive myself at last.

Phillip

Recovery! Forgiveness! I do not understand.

Mrs. Lattin

You have not **seen**. I understand for both of us.

Phillip

You have had dreams that troubled you. I implore you, dearest———

Mrs. Lattin

Look in my face. There is no trouble there—but only joy and life.

Phillip

Yes, yes, but—my darling, what *can* you mean?

Mrs. Lattin

He came—and went.

Phillip

And left one word behind him only———?

Mrs. Lattin

One word—Life.

Phillip

(*Almost convinced.*) Then—?

Mrs. Lattin

(*Radiant, rising from couch.*) I shall go back with you.

Phillip

To Egypt!

Mrs. Lattin

I shall never delay or thwart again. Ah, so many times I have—by my selfish love—(*breaks off*). Your work **is** a mission—always. It is your soul's career. I understand at last.

Phillip

Hush, hush, Little Child! You say wild things. I could never hear of it. I know your dread, your shrinking fear of Egypt. It would make you ill again. All the doctors agreed——

Mrs. Lattin

I have **no** dread! My shrinking was—a memory. It was instinctive—a cowardice that shirked sweet expiation—**there**, where it is due. (**In spite of him, she rises to her feet. Vigorous.**) I am well again. I shall go back with you. Your work—**my** work—lies out there—in Egypt. Oh, Phillip, be glad with me, for I am forgiven, I am healed!

Phillip

(*Stirred.*) Dear heart! Your soul is too grand for this frail, precious body. You injure yourself. Such sacrifice from you I could never, never——

[*Breaks off, as he notes the radiant expression in her face. They stand close together beneath the picture.*

Mrs. Lattin

(*Inflexibly.*) It is no sacrifice. It is love, love, love!

Phillip

(*Tenderly.*) That deep love I never doubted. But—the ingrained dread, the fear, the shrinking that have undermined your willing strength. How can you——?

Mrs. Lattin

They are gone for ever. Phillip, how often must I tell you? I am healed. I go back with you. We go together. Our life is there, in Egypt.

Phillip

(*Almost convinced.*) I feel some great new reality in you. You are most wonderfully changed. Some star of life is rising over us—again. (**He gazes into her radiant face with a touch of respect and wonder.**) If—if——

Mrs. Lattin

You must at once withdraw your resignation. There is no "too late"! (**Laughs a little.**) You promise me!

[*Amazement in him gives place to dawning belief at last. Yet he still hesitates.*

Phillip

I will see the doctor myself. I promise that if he——

Mrs. Lattin

You cannot.

Phillip

Cannot! (**Awe.**) You mean—you have had a vision?

Mrs. Lattin

He has—gone.

Phillip

(**Convinced.**) It **was** a vision…?

[*She turns slowly and looks up at the picture on the wall above them. He turns with her. He is speechless. He holds her very close. They stare together at the palms, the river, the stars, the temples.*

Mrs. Lattin

(**Softly.**) Egypt—where I first delayed and thwarted him, loving him for myself alone—Egypt, beneath your risen stars, beside your rising river—I **shall undo—at last**.

[*A new expression steals into his face. He gazes at the picture with her. He holds her still closer to him.*

Phillip

(**Moved and wondering.**) Little Child! It is very strange. Almost, it seems, some dream, some memory of long, long ago stirs in me.

[*A slight pause, as they gaze side by side at the picture.*

(**With effort.**) It is beyond me somewhere, but there is great beauty—that deep, unearthly Egyptian beauty in it. (**Lowers voice.**) Those palms are rustling, those stars seem to move, the Nile flows down towards the sea. Perhaps.... The Tear of Isis falls....

Mrs. Lattin

Listen ... yes...!

Phillip

(**Turns to her.**) Something about you, something new and—and familiar almost—steals upon me. I half believe....

Mrs. Lattin

(**Whispering.**) Phillip, my faithful one, I heard another name as you said that. I heard an ancient name—was it Menophis?

Phillip

(**Hushed voice.**) *I* thought a name came to me too. It floated past—Nefertiti. It must have been the beating of your heart against my own.

[*They stand motionless, gazing, listening.*

Mrs. Lattin

Dear, ancient names. How sweet they sound!

Phillip

(*Smiling.*) I think we are bewitched!

Mrs. Lattin

Egypt! (*Pause. Adds softly.*) I understand—at last.

[*He draws her head back and looks tenderly into her eyes.*

Phillip

All but one thing.

Mrs. Lattin

Which is——?

Phillip

That what you call delay has helped and taught me.

Mrs. Lattin

(*Low.*) Perhaps I understand that too. That which the soul can do without is added to it. (*Whispers.*) Is it not that?

Phillip

Ah, you put it so. Perhaps you put it better. I only know that you have given me the thing I needed most—perspective, the longer sight. My vision clears. (*Bends down and kisses her.*) I feel new power for my work. I see it whole.

Mrs. Lattin

Then my forgiveness is complete.

CURTAIN